IMAGES OF WAR

THE GILBERT AND ELLICE ISLANDS: PACIFIC WAR

RARE PHOTOGRAPHS FROM WARTIME ARCHIVES

Jim Moran

Pen & Sword
MILITARY

First published in Great Britain in 2019 by
PEN & SWORD MILITARY
An imprint of
Pen & Sword Books Ltd
47 Church Street
Barnsley
South Yorkshire
S70 2AS

ISBN 978-1-52675-119-5

Typeset by Concept, Huddersfield, West Yorkshire HD4 5JL.
Printed and bound by CPI Group (UK) Ltd, Croydon, CR0 4YY

Pen & Sword Books Limited incorporates the imprints of Atlas, Archaeology, Aviation, Discovery, Family History, Fiction, History, Maritime, Military, Military Classics, Politics, Select, Transport, True Crime, Air World, Frontline Publishing, Leo Cooper, Remember When, Seaforth Publishing, The Praetorian Press, Wharncliffe Local History, Wharncliffe Transport, Wharncliffe True Crime and White Owl.

For a complete list of Pen & Sword titles please contact
PEN & SWORD BOOKS LIMITED
47 Church Street, Barnsley, South Yorkshire S70 2AS, England
E-mail: enquiries@pen-and-sword.co.uk
Website: www.pen-and-sword.co.uk

'There were no cowards on Tarawa.'
General David M. Shoup, USMC

Contents

Introduction and Acknowledgements 6

Chapter One
The Gilbert and Ellice Islands: Pre Second World War . 7

Chapter Two
The Japanese Occupy the Gilbert Islands 11

Chapter Three
US Marine Raiders Assault Butaritari (Makin) 15

Chapter Four
Japanese Build-Up in the Gilbert Islands 39

Chapter Five
The United States Occupies the Ellice Islands 47

Chapter Six
The United States Assault on Tarawa, Makin and Apamama 59

Chapter Seven
The United States Occupies Makin and Tarawa 165

Appendix I
Casualties 171

Appendix II
Task Organization 173

Introduction and Acknowledgements

Days after the Japanese attack at Pearl Harbor, elements of the Japanese navy landed in the Gilbert Islands, in particular Makin, Tarawa and Apamama. The initial occupation of these atoll islands was low-key, with a seaplane facility being built on Butaritari (Makin) but no serious defences.

On 17 August 1942, Butaritari was attacked by elements of the US Marine 2nd Raider Battalion (Carlson's Raiders), landing in rubber boats launched from two submarines that had transported the 200-plus Raiders from Pearl Harbor. The Raiders eliminated almost the entire forty-four-man garrison and destroyed two radio stations and the seaplane tender, as well as storage and supply facilities on the island, before returning to the submarines and back to Hawaii.

The Makin Raid alerted the Japanese to the vulnerability of their outposts and work started in earnest to considerably increase the defences on, in particular, Makin, Tarawa and Apamama. Seaplane facilities were rebuilt on Makin, another seaplane facility was built on Apamama and an airfield was built on Betio (Tarawa). Defences were increased considerably, particularly on Betio, and garrison troops now numbered into the thousands.

In 1943, assaults on the Gilbert Islands by US forces (Operation GALVANIC) were given the 'green light'; in particular the taking of Tarawa (Betio), Apamama and Makin by US army and Marine troops. D-Day was set for 20 November 1943. The taking of these three islands was very costly in human lives, both US and Japanese; all three Japanese garrisons were eliminated almost to a man and US casualties were also severe, causing much concern back home in the US.

Following the islands being secured, US construction and garrison troops built airstrips on Tarawa and Makin but, due to the speed of the US advance across the Pacific, these facilities played little part in further operations in the Pacific.

Following the end of hostilities in the Pacific, the Gilbert and Ellice Islands were returned to British rule, finally gaining independence in 1979.

*　*　*

All images are courtesy of the US Army, US Navy and US Marine Corps unless otherwise stated. My thanks to all concerned.

Jim Moran

Chapter One

The Gilbert and Ellice Islands: Pre Second World War

The Gilbert and Ellice Islands had been a British protectorate since 1892, a peaceful sleepy Pacific paradise. Life was simple and the local population happy with life under British administration; the men were well-built and were expert seafarers with a profound knowledge of tides and a remarkable skill in navigating by the stars at night; they were also expert at gathering palm trees and coconuts for their British administration. The women were comely and industrious, with much of the heavy work being done by them.

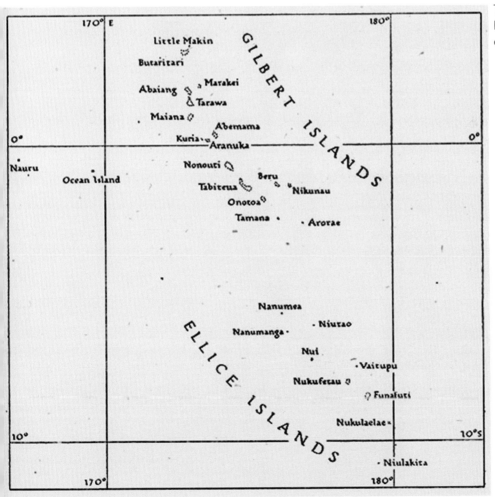

The Gilbert and Ellice Islands from Admiralty charts.

This detailed knowledge of tides had been passed on to British seafaring captains, who in turn would provide valuable information to the US planners for the invasion of the Gilbert Islands (the uncertain tides at Betio in particular). With the arrival of the Japanese in December 1941 life changed little at first, the local population carrying on much as normal until the raid on Makin by Carlson's Raiders in August 1942. After the Makin Raid the Japanese started a huge programme of defensive works using local labour, both male and female, in construction work. In 1942 the US established air bases and PT boat moorings in the Ellice Islands to monitor Japanese progress in the Gilberts and carry out pre-invasion bombing of Tarawa, Makin and Apamama in particular.

Coconuts, one of the main commodities on the islands.

Bounty of the sea: giant clams and oysters abound in the waters off the islands.

Visiting ships always attract much attention from the locals.

Gilbert Islands police; the only guns on the islands before the arrival of the Japanese.

Chapter Two

The Japanese Occupy the Gilbert Islands

On 9/10 December 1941, just three days after the surprise attack by the Japanese on the US Pacific Fleet at Pearl Harbor, elements of the Japanese Imperial Navy arrived at the Gilbert Islands. Comprising the 19th Minelayer Division, 29th Destroyer Division and elements of the 8th Gunboat Division, the objective of this attack force was to secure Tarawa Atoll first, then join the attack force at Makin Atoll.

At the same time, the Makin attack group consisting of the minelayer *Okinoshima Maru*, the auxiliary minelayer *Tenyo Maru* and I Company of the 51st Guard Force (Rikusentai, Japanese Marine Corps) arrived at Makin Atoll and commenced the occupation of Butaritari Island.

The Tarawa attack force landed its landing force of around 200 men, who proceeded to round up all non-islander people, informing them that they were now under the 'protection' of His Imperial Majesty. Under no circumstances were they to attempt to leave the islands or communicate with the outside world under pain of death (however, several would escape in a boat missed by the attack force). The landing party then proceeded to ransack the islands, destroying any boats found, any radio equipment or anything else of use, looting anything they could use themselves; particularly foodstuffs from the Burns Philp warehouses. Confident that they had achieved their objectives, the attack force returned to their ships and headed for Makin. They had neglected to locate several Australian and New Zealand army coast-watchers who remained for some time until their capture after the Makin Raid by Carlson's Raiders in August 1942.

Meanwhile, in the early hours of 10 December the Makin attack force debarked their landing force troops and had the island secured by 0800 hours. Two hours later the *Nagata Maru* arrived and proceeded to offload building materials for the seaplane facility. The facility was completed in two days.

On 11 December the *Okinoshima Maru* departed Butaritari to land the small force of Rikusentai on Little Makin, 6 miles to the north, then returned to Kwajalein Island. With the flying boat facility complete, all vessels returned to Kwajalein (with several prisoners), leaving a detachment of the 51st Guard Force assigned to guard the seaplane base. This guard force was reorganized into the 62nd Guard Force, Makin Dispatched Landing Force, on 10 April 1942 under the command of Warrant Officer Kanemitsu. This unit on Makin dwindled in numbers so that by August 1942 it was down to just forty-four combat troops when Carlson's Raiders arrived.

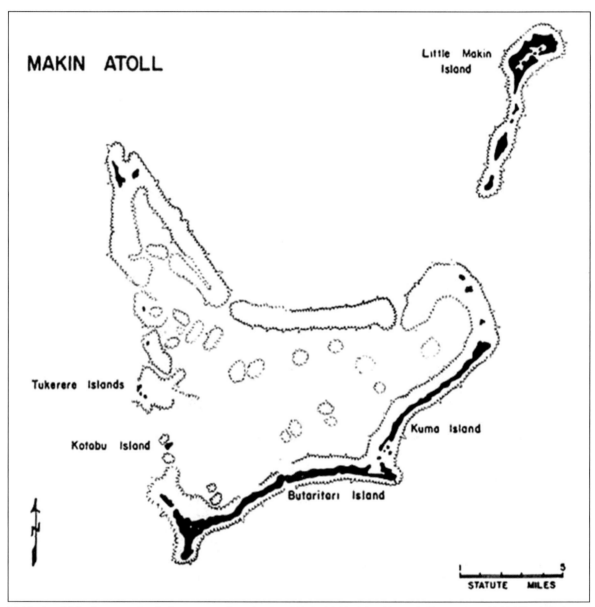

Makin Atoll. The Japanese landed troops on Butaritari and Little Makin Island in early December 1941. The US always referred to the islands as 'Makin Island', even though combat was only on Butaritari and Little Makin.

Declaration

The Empire of Japan declared war on America Britain and Dutch Indies to break down these hostilities on Dec. 8th and Japanese Naval Forces have occupied Gilbert Islands to day in the morning. It is our duty to secure the military supremacy in to our hands but we have never enmity for the Gilbert peoples. Accordingly the peoples to do the peaceful conduct will be protected sufficiently, but if you will do hostile acts or do not submit my order, you will be punished with heavy penalties.

December 10th 1941
Commander of Japanese Squadron

Declaration posted on Tarawa, 10 December 1941 (the original is kept in the Australian Archives, Canberra).

Mitsubishi F1M ('Pete'), Makin Island. The seaplane facilities on Butaritari (Makin) were used by Mitsubishi F1M ('Pete') seaplanes, among others, for refuelling while carrying out reconnaissance over areas around Makin and Tarawa (including the Ellice Islands).

Kawanishi H8K ('Emily') flying boat. These used the facilities at Makin, one landing reinforcements during the raid by Carlson's Raiders on Makin, which was destroyed by gunfire from the Raiders. The remains are still to be seen in the lagoon to this day.

Chapter Three

US Marine Raiders Assault Butaritari (Makin)

In the early hours of 17 August 1942, two submarines surfaced offshore of the island of Butaritari, Makin Island. The two submarines were the USS *Nautilus* (SS-168) and the USS *Argonaut* (SS-166). On board were 222 men of the US Marine 2nd Raider Battalion (Carlson's Raiders). The Raiders had boarded the submarines in Pearl Harbor, Hawaii in the early hours of 8 August and the two submarines departed at around 0900 hours on separate courses for Makin. At this time the Raiders (other than Lieutenant Colonel Evans Carlson and his Executive Officer James Roosevelt – the US president's eldest son) had no idea of their objective.

The 2,000-mile journey had been uneventful, both submarines making the bulk of the journey on the surface, allowing the Raiders brief time on deck for fresh air and a little exercise. It was not until the last day, 16 August, that the Raiders learned the name of their objective: 'Makin Island' (actually Butaritari).

Both submarines remained submerged until 0300 hours on 17 August when they surfaced and deck hatches opened to be greeted by atrocious conditions. Major General Oscar Peatross, then a first lieutenant, described the scene:

> The *Nautilus* surfaced on schedule, the hatches were opened and we were met by weather conditions for which the adjective was 'atrocious'. Rain was coming down in torrents, a strong wind was whipping up whitecaps. Seas were running high and the submarine was rolling and pitching heavily. As the Marines prepared to go ashore, two rubber boats containing machine guns, ammunition and medical supplies were swept away.

The assaulting Raiders were to make the final few hundred yards by rubber boats (LCR(L)), which were stowed aboard the two submarines and had to be hauled on deck and inflated. These were intended to be inflated on deck, loaded with men and equipment and when ready the submarine would submerge sufficiently to allow the rubber boats to cast off. Unfortunately, due to the prevailing weather conditions this was impossible to achieve, so the boats were inflated and launched over the sides of the two submarines, the Raiders jumping down from the decks into the boats below. Not an easy task and a miracle that no-one was badly hurt.

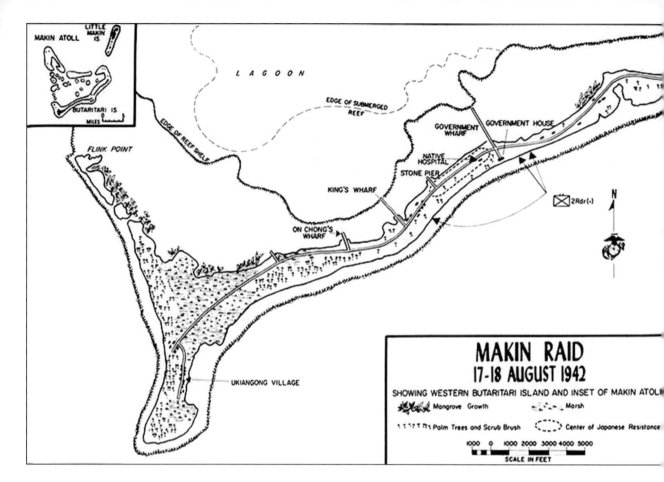

MAKIN RAID
17-18 AUGUST 1942

SHOWING WESTERN BUTARITARI ISLAND AND INSET OF MAKIN ATOLL

Mangrove Growth · Marsh
Palm Trees and Scrub Brush · Center of Japanese Resistance

1000 0 1000 2000 3000 4000 5000
SCALE IN FEET

By 0330 hours all the boats were loaded and ready to go; they all rendezvoused alongside the *Nautilus*, which still had Carlson and his runner aboard. Lieutenant Peatross collected Carlson and his runner in his boat and before transferring them both onto another boat, allowing him to return and check for stragglers. By the time Peatross had finished his checks, the main body of boats had set out for the island. Finding himself and his boat crew alone, Peatross got a bearing from the *Nautilus* and struck out alone for the island, landing approximately a mile to the south-west of the main body of men. It was originally intended for Company A to land on Beach Y and Company B to land on Beach Z; however, the main body had all landed on Beach Z with the exception of two boats: one of Company A which landed 200 yards south-west of Beach Z and one of Company B which landed approximately a mile north-east of Beach Z. Both crews of these two boats would link up with the main body, but Lieutenant Peatross and his men would fight their own battle, never linking up with the others.

At 0543 hours, Carlson radioed the *Nautilus* 'Everything lousy', but by 0600 hours Company A and Company B were organized and all stragglers on board (except Lieutenant Peatross and his men), allowing Carlson to radio 'Situation improved'.

Now reorganized into Companies A and B, Carlson ordered Company A under Lieutenant Plumley to advance across the island to the lagoon side (on the original plan of attack, this was to be Company B). The change caused some confusion, but Lieutenant Plumley dropped a man off every 50 yards as guides for Company B Captain Coyte to follow. Some of the Company B men actually passed Company A crossing the island and this would cause more confusion shortly. Company A reached the lagoon side, identifying the bomb-damaged Government Wharf, and set up defensive positions by Government House. As men of Company A approached Government House, they were fired upon by what turned out to be men from Company B who had overtaken Company A and occupied Government House. Luckily no-one was injured.

Local natives, now roused, informed Carlson where the most part of the Japanese defences were situated, around On Chong Wharf, also that the Japanese had been on high alert since the US landings on Guadalcanal. The natives also told Carlson that the Japanese garrison numbered between 80 and 200; 80 was much nearer the actual figure but Carlson chose to err on the side of caution and accept the higher figure.

First Platoon, Company A under Second Lieutenant LeFrançois moved out, advancing towards the Japanese defences down both sides of the lagoon road. Contact with the Japanese was made when approximately 300 yards ahead of the Raiders a truck pulled up on the road and some twenty Japanese Rikusentai jumped out, planted a flag and disappeared into the brush on either side of the road. Shortly after this, more Japanese troops arrived to join the first truckload in the brush. The Raiders dispersed into a defensive position and as the Japanese began to advance across open ground Second Lieutenant LeFrançois swung his left flank inward, creating a pocket for the unsuspecting Japanese to walk into. Sergeant Thomason's squad opened fire first, followed by the rest of the Company A Raiders.

Most of the Japanese advancing across open ground were cut down, but the Raiders still received fire from machine guns in the brush and snipers concealed in the tops of palm trees. This was the first time US troops encountered snipers in tree-tops. Most of the Raiders' fatalities or wounds would be at the hands of the snipers, including Sergeant Thomason, later awarded the Medal of Honor, the first enlisted Marine to receive the award in the Second World War.

After half an hour things quietened down with the exception of the occasional sniper, and Carlson ordered 1st Platoon Company B to reinforce the lagoon side flank. Unbeknown to him, the bulk of the Japanese defenders were now dead, but Carlson still believed the 200 figure given to him by locals. Raider casualties continued to mount from snipers and Carlson ordered 2nd Platoon Company B up to reinforce Company A. This situation remained until 1130 hours when shouts and bugles were heard and the Raiders encountered their first Banzai charge. The Japanese were cut down en masse at the cost of six Raiders killed. Carlson was unaware that there was now only a handful of Japanese still alive.

While 'the battle of the breadfruit trees' was going on, Lieutenant Peatross and his eleven men were having a battle of their own. Having crossed the island and orientated themselves, they advanced upon hearing all the gunfire in the direction of what they hoped would be the bulk of the Raiders. Peatross sent two runners forward by different routes to try to make contact with Carlson. One runner returned, having been unable to get through enemy lines; the other made it to Carlson's command post, telling Carlson of Peatross's location to the Japanese rear. Carlson thanked the runner, who remained at Carlson's CP but made no attempt to contact Peatross. Peatross continued to advance on the Japanese rear, killing one Japanese coming out of their barracks building and two others attempting to escape on bicycles. As Peatross and his men approached the Japanese HQ building, a man 'wearing a pith helmet, white shirt and khaki shorts' ran out. He fell in a hail of bullets. What Peatross and his men did not know was that they had just killed the island commander, Warrant Officer Kanemitsu.

With still no word from Carlson, Peatross and his men continued to advance, killing any Japanese they encountered and destroying anything of value to the enemy. They were within 400 yards of the main Raider body but never linked up with Carlson.

Shortly after arriving on the lagoon side of the island, two vessels were spotted moored close to On Chong Wharf. At 07.10 Major Roosevelt requested a fire mission of the *Nautilus* on the two vessels. Lacking coordinates and with direct view being obscured by palm trees, the *Nautilus* saturated the area with 6in shells and unbelievably sank both vessels. Locals informed Carlson that there were sixty troops on the two vessels (in fact there were none), but Carlson remained worried about the number of Japanese troops he was facing.

At 11.30 the Raiders heard aircraft engines and two Nakajima E6N2 ('Dave') reconnaissance floatplanes were observed overhead. Both submarines had detected the planes and had submerged to safety. The two planes circled the island for fifteen minutes, dropped two bombs and departed. At 12.55 the *Nautilus'* radar detected twelve approaching aircraft and at 13.20 two Kawanishi H8K1 ('Emily') flying boats, four Kawanishi E7K1 ('Alf') reconnaissance floatplanes, four Mitsubishi A6M ('Archie') Zero fighters and two Nakajima E6N2 floatplanes attacked, dropping bombs and strafing for one and a half hours. The Raiders had been trained to take cover and not return fire on aircraft and suffered only a few minor wounded. Their mission complete, ten of the twelve aircraft departed for home but two others – one 'Emily' and one 'Dave' – landed in the lagoon and proceeded to taxi towards On Chong Wharf. Upon seeing this, Company A Platoon Sergeant Victor 'Transport' Maghakian directed three machine guns and two Boys anti-tank guns to fire on the approaching aircraft. The 'Dave' was hit several times and burst into flames, sinking immediately.

The 'Emily' was riddled with .30 calibre and .55 calibre rounds but managed to turn and take off, lifting briefly but crashing back into the lagoon in flames. The 'Emily' being capable of carrying up to forty-one troops, Carlson was concerned that more Japanese had arrived, not helped when locals informed him that thirty-seven troops had escaped from the burning 'Emily'. The wreckage of this aircraft remains in the lagoon on Butaritari to this day.

With the bulk of the fighting over, except for the occasional sniper, Carlson was faced with a choice of continuing with the original plan to eliminate the Japanese garrison and destroy everything of potential use or preparing to return to the sub-marines. Still thinking that the Japanese numbered 200-plus and with a body count of less than 100, Carlson prepared to return to the submarines; in fact, there were fewer than 20 Japanese still alive.

Air attacks continued through the afternoon, but caused few casualties to the Raiders. At 16.00 Carlson ordered the centre and right to retire, leaving the left flank to cover the centre and right in case of any Japanese advance into the vacated posi-tions. Some Japanese did advance into the vacated Raider centre; these were fired upon from Japanese aircraft that strafed the area at 16.30. At around 17.00 Carlson sent a detail back to the landing beach to ready the rubber boats for departure. With one squad acting as a rearguard, the rubber boats began to load with men, starting with the fourteen wounded. It was intended that the withdrawal would start at around 19.30 under cover of darkness.

At 19.30 Carlson gave the order to launch boats, the middle two being for Carlson and the rearguard. The Raiders waded into chest-deep water carrying the boats before climbing on board. With all boats launched, Carlson ordered the last two into the water. With Carlson being the last man in – or so he thought – the rearguard did not receive the order to retire to the boats and were left stranded, unbeknown to all, including Carlson.

Few of the outboard motors worked so everyone paddled, but they were making very little headway against the rolling breakers coming at them. Many boats were capsized or swamped, men and equipment being tossed overboard, the wounded suffering most. Few of the vessels made it into open water; only four boats with fifty-three Raiders made it to the *Nautilus*, with three boats and twenty-seven Raiders reaching the *Argonaut*. The first boat to reach the *Nautilus* was greeted by Lieutenant Peatross, much to their surprise. Peatross and his eight-man squad had retired to their boat as per the original plan. After observing the waves for a time and determining that every fifth wave was the smallest, they concluded this was the time to launch their boat. This they did; even the outboard motor cooperated by bursting into life. Peatross and his crew made it through the breakers easily and after one hour arrived alongside the *Nautilus*.

In contrast, the main body of Raiders had tried time after time to navigate a way through the breakers but was repeatedly washed back to the beach. Carlson directed his remaining Raiders to recover what arms and equipment they could find and he pulled the covering force back to form a line of defence around the exhausted men on the beach. At 23.00 the perimeter force was attacked by eight Japanese, three of whom were killed and one of the Raiders was badly wounded. This reinforced Carlson's concerns that there was still a number of Japanese left fighting on the island. At 00.00 Carlson called an officers' meeting to review the situation. It was at this meeting that the possibility of surrender was raised. It is alleged that at 03.30 Carlson sent Captain Coyte and Private McCall out with a note proposing surrender. A lone Japanese – probably one of the eight that attacked the perimeter guard – was found, was given the note and told to take it to his commanding officer. The Japanese took off and shortly afterwards shots were heard; the lone Japanese had been shot by other Raiders, unaware of what was happening. Coyte and McCall returned to Carlson to inform him of their failure to deliver the surrender note. Following the Japanese return to Makin they claimed to have found the note on the body of a Japanese sailor and broadcast its content over 'Tokyo Rose' propaganda radio. After the war no note was found but the question of its existence remains to this day. Most of Carlson's Raiders who were on the raid flatly refuse to believe Carlson would have even considered surrender. Another factor to consider was that Major Roosevelt (the president's son) was still on the island and Carlson could not allow him to be captured. In his after-action report, Carlson would refer to this time as his 'spiritual low point'.

Carlson had decided to attempt to vacate the island from the lagoon side the next day. It would have to be after dark as the two submarines would need to remain submerged during the day. This meant that the Raiders would have to endure possible counter-attacks and air attacks during the day. At dawn on 18 August Carlson informed his men of the intention of crossing the island and escaping to the waiting submarines through the lagoon, some 2 miles across open water. Any men who wished to escape surf-side were free to do so; the submarines would be waiting for them. Four boats made it through the surf to the waiting submarines – two to the *Nautilus* and two to the *Argonaut* – with around fifty men on board. One of the two boats to reach the *Argonaut* carried Major Roosevelt, who had been told by Carlson to take command of the Raiders on board the two submarines, thus eliminating one major concern which was the safety of the president's son. Carlson's intentions were relayed to the Task Group Commander, Commander Haines, aboard the *Nautilus*. Lieutenant Peatross had made a request to take a boat back to the breaker line with a line-throwing gun to fire a rescue line onto the beach and allow the remaining men stranded on the beach to escape. His request had been denied earlier by Haines, but now Haines allowed Peatross to send a five-man team by boat back to the island.

Five volunteers led by Sergeant Allard set off from the *Nautilus* shoreward. They reached the breaker line, and one man swam to the beach and informed Carlson that the submarines would be waiting for them at the lagoon entrance at 19.30 before swimming back to the rescue boat. At the same time the first air attack came over the island, bombing and strafing, including the rescue boat which was riddled and sank. None of the five men on board was seen again; they all survived the attack but were left behind on the island, captured along with four other Raiders who had been left behind when the Japanese returned to Makin in force and were later executed on Kwajalein.

Things were, however, looking better for Carlson, who was still on the beach with around thirty men, some of whom were wounded. He called everyone together for a 'gung ho' talk, informing them all of his intention to get off the island after dark that night. To keep the men occupied, Carlson sent out scouting parties for food, clothing, arms and ammunition, both American and Japanese. Carlson himself toured the previous day's battlefield, noting the dead Raiders, laying them out as best he could and saying a prayer over each of them. Without tools to bury them, Carlson asked the native chief of police, Joe Miller, to give his men a decent burial, giving him $50 and several weapons and ammunition. This Miller promised to do.

During the day the Raiders endured four more air-raids but suffered no casualties. The Raiders destroyed the Japanese radio station at On Chong Wharf and ignited 1,000 barrels of aviation fuel stored near King's Wharf. The Raiders even found time to collect a few souvenirs. Carlson sent Lieutenant Lamb with two men to check out a motorized sloop in the lagoon by the Japanese trading station. As the three approached the sloop in a rowing boat, a hand holding a pistol appeared at a port-hole and fired but missed them. They returned fire by dropping a hand grenade through the porthole, killing the lone Japanese sailor guarding the sloop. On close inspection, the sloop was taking on water badly and it was decided that it would be of no use to the Raiders. The Raiders commandeered a native outrigger canoe and lashed their four remaining serviceable rubber boats to it, fitting the only two working motors to the outer boats. On schedule, the two submarines surfaced at the lagoon entrance at 19.30 and awaited contact with Carlson on shore, receiving a Morse code message from shore telling them that the Raiders should be with them at 23.00. The makeshift raft set out across the lagoon with all on board at 20.30, the wounded on stretchers laid across the canoe. The going was slow and one rubber boat crew requested to leave and make for the submarines alone. Carlson gave them permission to leave, which they did but they were never seen again. The number of men on this boat is unknown but it is thought that four of them were among those captured by the Japanese on Makin and subsequently executed on Kwajalein. The remainder of the Raiders reached the lagoon entrance by 22.00 and, spotting the marker lights on the two submarines, arrived at 23.08 alongside the submarines. Searchlights were switched on and willing sailors hauled the exhausted Raiders on board. As it was thought that all hands were now accounted for, the two submarines set a course for Hawaii. Radio silence being enforced, the final head count of Raiders would have to wait until arrival in Hawaii and it was after the end of the Second World War that it became known that nine Raiders had been left behind and later executed.

After an uneventful return trip the two submarines pulled into Pearl Harbor to a heroes' welcome, much to the amazement of Raiders and sailors alike, with the *Nautilus* arriving on 25 August and the *Argonaut* on the following day. On arrival, the Raiders and crew of the *Nautilus* were assembled on deck and greeted by all ships, with crews assembled on deck in dress whites, and on the quayside by cheering crowds of spectators, while Marine bands played the *Marine Hymn* and *Anchors Aweigh*. Marine and navy officers were on hand to congratulate Carlson on a job well done. The same reception was afforded the *Argonaut* on the following day. The Royal Hawaiian Hotel, an exclusive R&R centre for submarine crews, received the Raiders as guests of the *Nautilus* and *Argonaut* crews, who also presented the Raiders with the Submarine Combat Patrol pin, a unique honour.

Many tall tales were told and souvenirs displayed; Major Roosevelt went to Washington DC to brief his father (the president) and present him with a Japanese flag taken from Makin. Even Hollywood got in on the act, making the film *Gung Ho!* in 1943 with three of the Makin Raiders as advisors, namely Lieutenant Colonel Carlson, Lieutenant Wilfred LeFrançois and Sergeant Victor 'Transport' Maghakian.

(**Opposite, above**) Members of 2nd Raider Battalion, USMC: 'Carlson's Raiders', named after their commanding officer, Lieutenant Colonel Evans F. Carlson, USMC. These men were highly-trained in Commando tactics and were all volunteers.

(**Opposite, below**) USS *Nautilus* (SS-168) and USS *Argonaut* (SS-166): the two submarines used to transport Company A and Company B, 2nd Raider Battalion from Hawaii to Makin Island and back, a journey of more than 2,000 miles each way.

USS *Nautilus*: on board were, in addition to a crew of eight officers and eighty-eight enlisted men, the Task Group Commander, Commander Robert Haines, and seventy-nine men of Company B, 2nd Raider Battalion, plus six Raiders from the Command Group including Lieutenant Colonel Carlson and his Intelligence Officer, First Lieutenant Holtom.

USS *Argonaut*: along with the USS *Nautilus*, the *Argonaut* had on board the remainder of 27 men from Company B in addition to 106 men from Company A with Major James Roosevelt and Demolitions Officer Captain Davis, along with Company A Commander First Lieutenant Plumley and Company B Commander Captain Coyte. This made a total task force of 222 officers and men from the 2nd Raider Battalion, USMC. Unfortunately, while attacking a Japanese convoy en route to Rabaul on 10 January 1943, the *Argonaut* was detected and depth-bombed. Forced to surface, the *Argonaut* came under fire from three Japanese destroyers and was lost with all 102 hands.

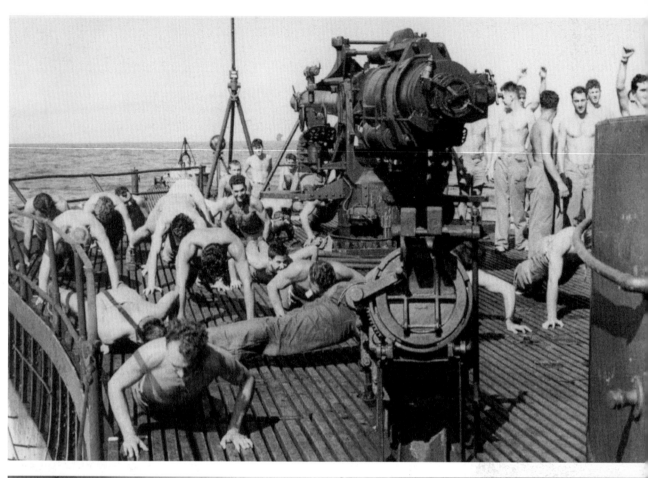

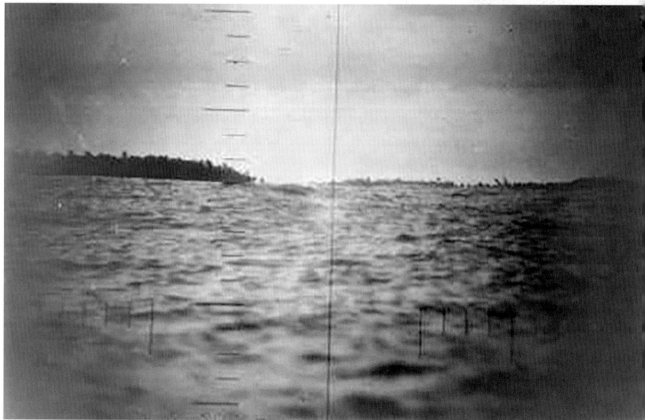

(**Opposite, above**) An uneventful journey from Hawaii to Makin. Most of the journey was taken on the surface by the submarines; this allowed brief time on deck for the Raiders exercising on the gun deck of the USS *Nautilus*.

(**Opposite, below**) Makin Island (Butaritari) as seen through the periscope of the USS *Nautilus* on arrival on 16 August.

(**Above**) LCR(L) Landing Craft Rubber (Large) to be used by the Raiders from the submarines to shore. Carried deflated in the submarine torpedo storage area, these rubber boats had to be hauled on deck, inflated, loaded and launched into a heaving Pacific Ocean several hundred yards from the island in far from favourable conditions.

Getting all the Raiders on deck from below was not an easy task. All weapons were unloaded only to be loaded when the enemy was detected. Equipment was minimal: only ammunition, weapon, 'D' ration chocolate bar and a few personal items carried in a Mk. IV A1 gas mask bag as seen here.

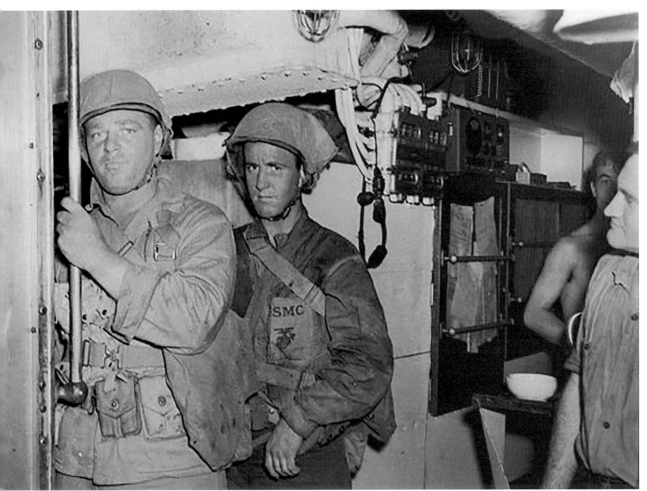

Waiting to go topside on the USS *Nautilus*, two Raiders – Sergeant Walter Carroll and Private First Class Dean Winters – wait by the open deck hatch. Carroll and Winters formed one of the two Boys anti-tank gun teams on the raid. Carroll stopped a truck on the lagoon side road with a round to the truck's radiator, the occupants taken under fire as they exited the burning truck. Carroll also put several rounds into the 'Emily' flying boat, causing it to crash into the lagoon (the 'Emily' is still to be seen in the lagoon to this day).

Lieutenant Colonel Evans Fordyce Carlson, seen here after returning to the USS *Nautilus* on the evening of 18 August, said by one person to have 'aged ten years over the last two days'.

(**Above**) Major James Roosevelt, Carlson's Executive Officer and second-in-command on the Makin Raid. The eldest son of President F.D. Roosevelt, his safety on the Makin Raid was always foremost in Carlson's mind. Carlson had promised President Roosevelt that no harm would come to his son, but James Roosevelt was determined to do his part in the raid to the full, which he did.

(**Opposite, above**) One of several photographs taken unofficially on the Makin Raid by Ray Bauml. Taken outside the local school house, it shows two Raiders taking time for a cigarette. Raider Mel Spotts took a camera and ten rolls of film along on the raid but none of it survived to get off the island. Ray Bauml was more successful.

(**Opposite, below left**) Ray Bauml photograph, again taken outside the local school house.

(**Opposite, below right**) Private Alden C. Mattison photographed by Ray Bauml outside the local school house just hours before Mattison was killed in action by a Japanese sniper.

(**Left**) Sergeant Clyde Thomason – one of the first Raiders to fall in 'the battle of the breadfruit trees' – was the first enlisted Marine to receive the Medal of Honor in the Second World War. His citation reads: 'For conspicuous gallantry and intrepidity at the risk of his life above and beyond the call of duty while a member of the Second Marine Raider Battalion in action against the Japanese-held island of Makin on August 17–18, 1942. Landing the advance element of the assault echelon, Sergeant Thomason disposed his men with keen judgement and discrimination and by his exemplary leadership and great personal valor, exhorted them to like fearless efforts. On one occasion, he dauntlessly walked up to a house which concealed an enemy Japanese sniper, forced in the door and shot the man (with a trench gun) before he could resist. Later in the action, while leading an assault on enemy positions, he gallantly gave up his life in the service of his country. His courage and loyal devotion to duty in the face of grave peril were in keeping with the finest traditions of the United States Naval Service.

(**Right**) Raider Dean Winters safely back on board the USS *Nautilus*. Many of the Raiders had lost weapons, equipment and even clothes while attempting to get off the island. Here Winters had armed himself on the second day with a Japanese rifle and ammunition belt.

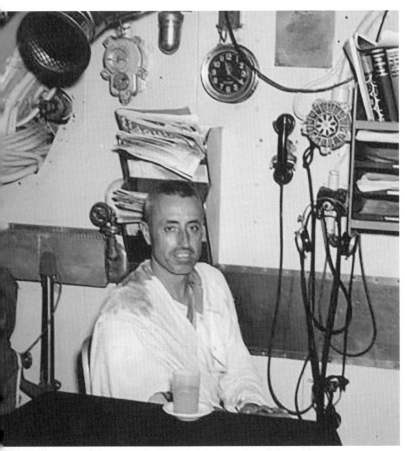

Lieutenant Wilfred S. LeFrançois suffered five machine-gun bullets to his right arm and shoulder during 'the battle of the breadfruit trees'. It was LeFrançois' story of the Makin Raid written in December 1942 for the *Saturday Evening Post* that formed the basis of the script for Hollywood's 1943 film *Gung Ho!*. LeFrançois, Carlson and 'Transport' Maghakian were technical advisors to the film.

Safely back at Hawaii, the USS *Nautilus* docks at Pearl Harbor to a hero's welcome. Both crew and Raiders man the decks, the Raiders dressed in anything they could find, including Marine dungarees, 'black khakis' and navy dungarees loaned by the crew.

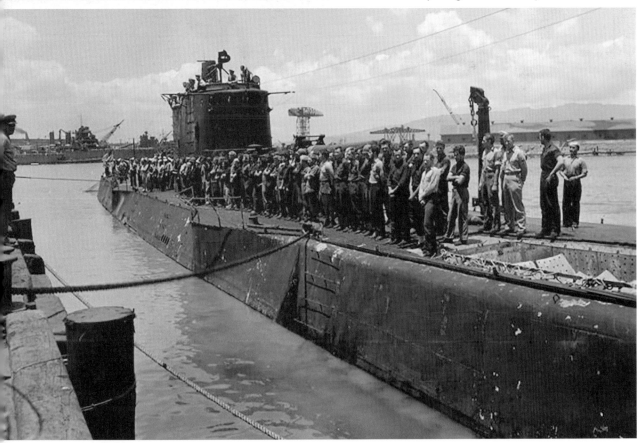

Home safe at Hawaii. Raiders and crew pose for the cameras. Most of the Raiders wear their 'black khakis': summer khaki shirt and trousers that they had dyed black for the night landing on Makin, but when confronted with foul weather on arrival most of the Raiders opted to wear their HBT (Herringbone Twill) dungarees. Unfortunately many Raiders lost their clothes as well as their equipment while attempting to get off the island.

Lieutenant Colonel Carlson and Major Roosevelt being congratulated by fellow Marine officers on a job well done.

First Lieutenant Oscar Peatross (centre), together with eleven men, conducted his own battle on Makin, never joining up with the main force throughout.

Lieutenant Colonel Carlson and Major Roosevelt display a souvenir Japanese flag taken on the Makin Raid. Major Roosevelt travelled to Washington DC to present the flag to his father, President Franklin D. Roosevelt.

Dr S.L. Stigler, Lieutenant USN (far left), along with Dr W.B. McCracken, Lieutenant USN, both received Navy Crosses for their work on the wounded Raiders on Makin.

Left to right: Lieutenant LeFrançois, Lieutenant Colonel Carlson and Sergeant Victor 'Transport' Maghakian on the set of the film *Gung Ho!*. All three were technical advisors on the film, based on the account of LeFrançois in the *Saturday Evening Post*.

Marine poster for the 1943 film *Gung Ho!*, hailed as a 'true account' of the Makin Raid.

LCR(L) used by Carlson's Raiders transferring from the two submarines onto and off Makin Island (Butaritari).

Main Inflation Manifold

Inflation Valves for Pneumatic Deck

Carbon – Dioxide Bottle

Inflation Valves for Cross Tubes

Topping – Off Valve

Machine – Gun Mount Patches

Spray Tube

Optional Manifold

Spray Tube Valv

Motor Mount

Spray Tube Valv

Pelican Hook

Motor-Tool Pocket

Bridle Lines

Life Line

Carrying Handles

Towing Howser

Pop-Off Valve

Pump Pocket

Repair Pockets

Pressure Guage

Quick – Release Line

Machine – Gun Mount

Carrying Handles

Motor Mount

Pelican Hook

Bridle Lines

D-Ring

Dry deck launch for LCR(L)s from submarines. This was the launch type used by Carlson's Raiders due to the weather conditions. The alternative wet deck launch was preferred by the Raiders.

Wet deck launch of LCR(L) preferred by the Raiders, but weather conditions prevented this type of launch.

After the Makin raid the Raiders were given free access to the Royal Hawaiian Hotel by the crew of the two submarines that carried the raiders to Makin and back. The Royal Hawaiian Hotel was intended to be for sole use of submarine crews on R&R in Hawaii, an honor indeed! Here two Raiders render a snappy salute for the cameras.

Chapter Four

Japanese Build-Up in the Gilbert Islands

Butaritari and the neighbouring islands were bombed by the Japanese on 19 August, the day after the Raiders had left to return to Hawaii. All, that is, except for the nine Raiders who did not get off the island back to the submarines, unbeknown to Carlson. These Raiders made their way to Little Makin and, with the assistance of a French priest, Father Clivaz, who gave them a native canoe, food and water, set sail on a 2,000-mile journey to Hawaii. Almost immediately after setting sail they were intercepted by a Japanese ship which took them on board and shipped them to Kwajalein, arriving on 2 September, where they were imprisoned. On 16 October 1942, the island commander, Vice Admiral Kōsō Abe, ordered the execution of all nine Raiders. They were taken away to the south-west end of Kwajalein, beheaded one by one and buried (Vice Admiral Abe was hanged for this crime in 1947).

On 20 August two 'Emily' flying boats delivered the first of 1,000 troops to Butaritari, who scoured the island burying the dead Raiders (buried by local natives who had promised Carlson they would do this) and cremating the Japanese dead, returning their ashes to Japan.

One of the main objectives of the Makin Raid was to divert troops from reinforcing those already engaged on Guadalcanal. This did not happen, but the raid did demonstrate to the Japanese high command how vulnerable was the outer line of defending islands and plans to reinforce these islands were put in place almost immediately.

On Makin, the Japanese soon rebuilt the seaplane facility, radio stations and storage facilities and then commenced building defensive works centred around On Chong Wharf, starting with huge tank traps east and west of the main defence area. Numerous machine-gun and anti-boat-gun emplacements were constructed on both lagoon and seaward sides of Butaritari and all were complete and manned by the time the US 27th Infantry arrived in November 1943.

Elsewhere on the Gilbert Islands, a further seaplane facility was constructed on Apamama with a small defence force of Rikusentai. On Tarawa, the main area of defence was going to be centred on Betio Island, at the extreme south-west end of

Tarawa Atoll. The Japanese high command had already decided that the main defence for the Gilberts was going to be Betio Island and a huge defensive construction programme was put into place, starting with the construction of an airstrip capable of facilitating the take-off and landing of Betty bombers.

The first troops to arrive on Tarawa were elements of the 6th Yokosuka SNLF (Special Naval Landing Force). These troops began building all-round defence works, although first of all a detachment was tasked with scouring Tarawa for any Allied coast-watchers. Several were rounded up and transported to Betio to be included with the local native labour force. These coast-watchers, mainly Australian and New Zealand Anzac personnel, were executed on Betio prior to the Allied invasion.

By the end of 1942 the Gilbert Islands had garrison troops of more than 1,500, mainly on Tarawa, Makin and Apamama. Defence works continued at a feverish pace, and garrison troops were augmented by the arrival of the 7th Sasebo SNLF in March 1943. Throughout 1943 and right up to the assault in November, defensive works continued, albeit hindered by Allied bombing and submarine activity. By the time Rear Admiral Keiji Shibasaki arrived on Betio to take command of the Gilbert Islands defence force, there were more than 4,500 personnel, mainly on Betio, although not all were combat troops.

At the time of the Allied invasion in November 1943, the Japanese had more than 500 fixed emplacements ranging from rifle pits to concrete gun emplacements for weapons up to 8in coastal guns. The four 8in coastal guns on the south-east and south-west corners of Betio (the so-called 'Singapore Guns' captured, it was believed, at Singapore by the Japanese), were, in fact, leftovers from the 1905 Russo-Japanese War, purchased by the Japanese from the English Vickers company.

(**Opposite, above**) Anti-tank gun emplacements like this one were part of the barrier defence system of the Japanese on Butaritari. Most were overrun by US forces before they could be manned (image taken after the island had been secured).

(**Opposite, below**) Section of an anti-tank ditch, situated at the east and west extremities of the main Japanese defence area on Butaritari. Some 6ft deep and over 14ft wide, these ditches ran partway across the island with both ends extended by log barriers, providing access into the main defence area.

Observation tower, Butaritari, built at the base of King's Wharf by the Japanese after the raid by Carlson's Raiders in August 1942. Japanese snipers took up positions during the assault in November 1943; these were cleared on D+1.

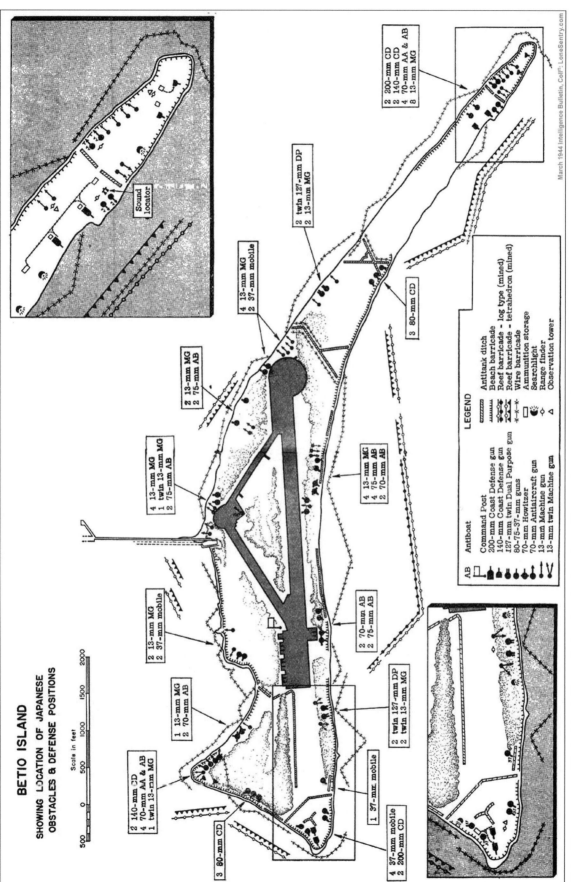

BETIO ISLAND

SHOWING LOCATION OF JAPANESE OBSTACLES & DEFENSE POSITIONS

Scale in feet

500 0 500 1000 1500 2000

Sound locator

2 twin 127-mm DP
2 13-mm MG

4 13-mm MG
2 37-mm mobile

2 13-mm MG
2 75-mm AB

4 13-mm MG
1 twin 13-mm MG
2 75-mm AB

2 13-mm MG
2 37-mm mobile

1 13-mm MG
2 70-mm AB

140-mm CD
4 70-mm AA & AB
1 twin 13-mm MG

3 80-mm CD

4 37-mm mobile
2 200-mm CD

2 twin 127-mm DP
2 twin 13-mm MG

1 37-mm mobile

4 13-mm MG
4 75-mm AB
2 70-mm AB

2 70-mm AB
2 75-mm AB

3 80-mm CD

2 200-mm CD
2 140-mm CD
4 70-mm AA & AB
8 13-mm MG

LEGEND

AB   Antiboat

☐	Command Post
	200-mm Coast Defense gun
	140-mm Coast Defense gun
	127-mm twin Dual Purpose gun
	80-75-37-mm guns
	70-mm Howitzer
	70-mm Antiaircraft gun
	13-mm Machine gun
	13-mm twin Machine gun

	Antitank ditch
	Beach barricade
	Reef barricade - log type (mined)
	Reef barricade - tetrahedron (mined)
	Wire barricade
	Ammunition storage
☼	Searchlight
	Range finder
△	Observation tower

March 1944 Intelligence Bulletin, Collⁿ. LoneSentry.com

US Intelligence map of Betio Island (Tarawa) showing the location of known Japanese obstacles and defence positions prior to the US assault in November 1943.

Japanese radio transmitting station situated in this heavily-revetted frame structure near the centre of Butaritari; it was the counterpart of a long-range receiving station located near King's Wharf. Both transmitter and receiver stations were rebuilt after the original stations were destroyed by Carlson's Raiders.

Beach barricade of logs on Betio Island. Note the heavily-constructed covered machine-gun emplacements. These took a heavy toll on the Marines on D-Day and D+2 (image taken after the battle).

Japanese Special Naval Landing Force (SNLF) troops mount one of the four British-made Vickers 8in guns into its turret on Betio. For years after the battle these four Vickers guns were referred to as the 'Singapore guns', wrongly thought to have come from Singapore after its surrender. These four guns were actually purchased from Vickers by the Japanese in 1905 during their war with Russia.

Rikusentai of the SNLF conduct pre-battle training on Betio Island (image from captured Japanese camera).

Rikusentai undergo field firing exercises prior to the November 1943 invasion (image from captured Japanese camera).

Chapter Five

The United States Occupies the Ellice Islands

In October of 1942 the US reaction to increased Japanese activity from the Gilbert Island bases towards the Ellice Islands was to commit forces to the Ellice Islands, in particular Funafuti, Nukufetau and Nanumea.

The 2nd Seabee Battalion landed at Funafuti on 2 October 1942, along with the 5th Marine Defence Battalion (Reinforced), consisting of an anti-aircraft battalion, two companies of infantry from the 3rd Marine Regiment and four OS2U Kingfisher observation floatplanes from Navy Scouting Squadron 65. On Funafuti the Seabees constructed an airstrip capable of use by B24 bombers, a seaplane facility and a PT boat dock (a four-boat PT squadron arrived in late 1942). The Seabees went on to construct airstrips on Nukufetau and Nanumea, manned initially by elements of the US 4th Marine Aircraft Wing. The two Air Groups comprised the following:

1. Marine Aircraft Group 13 (MAG13): Marine Fighting Squadron VMF-111, Marine Fighting Squadron VMF-441, Marine Torpedo Bombing Squadron VMSB-151 and Marine Scout Bombing Squadron VMSB-241.
2. Marine Aircraft Group 31 (MAG31): Marine Fighter Attack Squadron VMF-224, Marine Attack Squadrons VMF-311 and 321, Marine Attack Squadrons VMSB-331 and 341, and Marine Transport Unit VMJ-353.

These units were later augmented by B24 Liberator bombers of the US Army 7th Air Force. The Marine MAG13 and MAG31 aircraft were replaced by USAAF planes in November 1943. Reconnaissance missions were conducted over the Gilberts by the US from the Ellice Island bases starting in late 1942, and bombing missions were carried out throughout 1943, primarily on Tarawa during the lead-up to the 1943 invasion.

Early in 1943, Funafuti suffered several bombing raids by Japanese bombers from Nauru, Ocean Island and Tarawa, but there were few casualties or damage caused by these bombings. During the latter half of 1943, bombing missions increased, especially on Tarawa, in the build-up to Operation GALVANIC, the assault on the Gilbert Islands of Tarawa, Apamama and Makin scheduled for 20 November. Due to this increased activity, the Japanese transferred all serviceable aircraft from the Gilbert Islands to the Marshall Islands.

The Ellice Islands were to be the advance staging area for the invasion fleet heading for the Gilbert Islands.

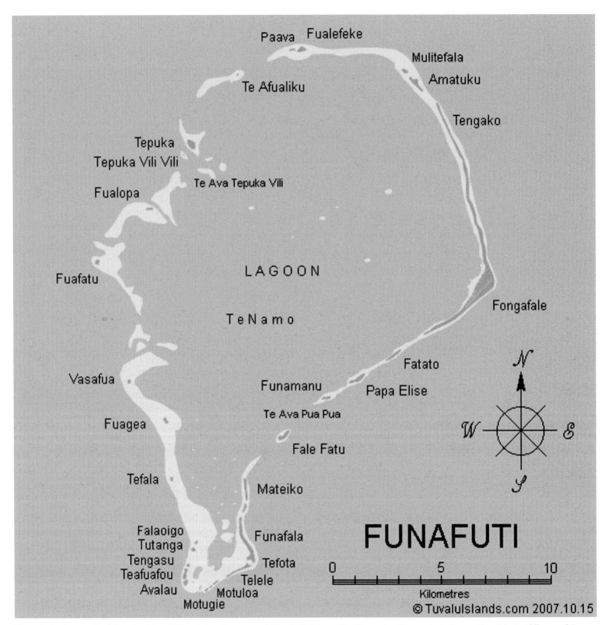

Funafuti, the main island of the Ellice Islands group. The US Navy Seabees built an airstrip on the islet of Fongafale, as well as a seaplane ramp and a PT boat station.

Elements of the US Marine 5th Defence Battalion were sent to Funafuti, Nukufetau and Nanumea. Their 90mm anti-aircraft guns were dual-purpose, being capable of engaging targets in the air and on the ground.

The 5th Defence Battalion anti-aircraft weapons had searchlights for night-time aerial defence. The Battalion was also equipped with SCR268 radar stationed on Funafuti.

Ageing M1918 155mm guns were the 5th Defence Battalion's main coastal defence weapons.

OS2U-2 Kingfisher: four of these from Navy Scouting Squadron 65 were the first planes to arrive in the Ellice Islands, stationed at the newly-built seaplane facility on Funafuti.

(**Above**) F4F Wildcats of VMF-224 (MAG31) were the first fighter aircraft to be stationed on the Ellice Islands' new air bases on Funafuti, Nukufetau and Nanumea. Two Air Wings – MAG13 and MAG31 – were eventually stationed on the Ellice Island bases, replaced in late 1943/early 1944 by USAAF 7th Air Force planes.

(**Opposite, above**) F4Fs of VMF-441 (MAG13) stationed at the airfield on Nanumea. These Wildcats were eventually replaced in 1944 by USAAF 7th Air Force planes along with VMF-224 (MAG31) Marine aircraft.

(**Opposite, below**) B24 Liberator bombers of the USAAF 7th Air Force stationed on Funafuti. These bombers were at the forefront of bombing operations against the Japanese-occupied islands in the Gilberts as well as other islands such as Ocean Island and Nauru Island throughout 1943 and 1944.

(**Above**) B24 Liberators of the USAAF 7th Air Force ready for another bombing mission, possibly against Tarawa or Makin.

(**Opposite, above**) B24 Liberator crews 'mount up' for another raid on Japanese-held islands.

(**Opposite, below**) PT boats of PT Squadron RON1, Division 2 at the newly-constructed dock on Funafuti, built on the lagoon side of Fongafale along with a seaplane ramp.

A PT boat undergoing repairs in dry dock facilities at the PT boat dock on Funafuti.

Douglas SBD Dauntless dive-bombers of UMA331 take off on another mission from their air base on Nanumea, Ellice Islands in November 1943.

An OS2U Kingfisher navy observation floatplane being recovered at the seaplane ramp on Funafuti Island. Four of these planes were based on Funafuti.

Chapter Six

The United States Assault on Tarawa, Makin and Apamama

At a conference in Hawaii in September 1943, plans were formulated for the advance across the central Pacific, 'island-hopping' to the eventual goal of capturing the Mariana Islands, which would put the Allies within bomber reach of Tokyo.

To reach the Marianas the Allies would first have to neutralize the Marshall Islands, approximately halfway between Hawaii and the Marianas. Recent events in the Gilbert Islands (Carlson's Makin Raid in August 1942) had made the Gilbert Islands a priority in the Japanese defence plans.

Operation GALVANIC, the invasion of Tarawa, Apamama and Makin Islands, was approved. Tarawa and Apamama were the targets for the US Marine 2nd Division (at that time recuperating in New Zealand after their involvement in Guadalcanal). Makin Island was the target for the US Army's 27th Infantry Division. Overall commander in the field was to be Marine Major General Holland M. Smith, whose explosive temper earned him the nickname 'Howlin' Mad' Smith, as the US Army's 27th Division commander was to find out on Makin.

The overall operation was under the command of three 'Smiths'. Holland M. Smith commanded the 5th Amphibious Corps, Major General Julian Smith commanded the 2nd Marine Division and Major General Ralph Smith, US Army, commanded the US Army's 27th Infantry Division.

The date for the invasion was set for 20 November 1943. Overall planning for the operation was under Colonel David M. Shoup. One of his main worries was the depth of the water over the barrier reef at the time of landing on 20 November. To assist him, Shoup had advisors who had lived on Betio/Tarawa and knew the tides well; one in particular, British Major Frank Holland, who had lived on Tarawa for fifteen years and had studied the tide patterns. He was appalled when he was told the date of 20 November as he knew there would be a 'dodging' tide with no more than 3ft of water over the reef, not enough for the LCVP (Landing Craft Vehicle Personnel) to get over it. Shoup's answer to the insufficiency of water over the reef was simple: they would use the amphibious tractors (LVTs, Landing Vehicles Tracked) that would take the first three waves of assault troops in them, return to the reef and carry out a shuttle service for the subsequent waves of troops. What Shoup did not allow for was that 50 per cent of the LVTs would be disabled within the first few hours of the invasion.

Final rehearsals for the invasion of Tarawa were carried out at Efate, New Hebrides, and it was here that Regimental Landing Team 2's designated leader Colonel William Marshall suffered a heart attack and Colonel Shoup was placed in command in his stead. Shoup was the highest-ranking officer to land on D-Day on Betio and, although wounded, assumed overall command on the beachhead until relieved by Colonel Merritt Edson, the divisional chief of staff. Shoup, however, remained on the island for the duration of the battle as Edson's assistant, in spite of his wounds. Shoup would later receive the Medal of Honor for devotion to duty on Tarawa and would eventually become commandant of the Marine Corps in 1959.

Just after midnight on 20 November the invasion fleet, the largest yet assembled in the Pacific for a single operation, consisting of eighteen aircraft carriers, twelve battleships, eight heavy cruisers, four light cruisers, sixty-six destroyers and thirty-six transport ships, hove to off the coast of Betio. B24 bombers of the 7th USAAF from Funafuti had been bombing Tarawa and Betio in particular for weeks prior to the invasion fleet's arrival. It had been planned that prior to troops landing on the beaches, the B24s would carry out saturation bombing on Betio with 500lb 'Daisy Cutter' bombs (fused to detonate a few feet above ground, acting as anti-personnel weapons). However, the B24s never arrived, claiming that bad weather prevented them from taking off; this was the first of several SNAFUs ('situation normal, all fouled up') on D-Day.

By 0300 hours transports were in position and troop-loading into LCVPs and LVTs commenced. At 04.41 a single red star shell shot skyward from the blacked-out island; there were definitely Japanese there! At 05.00 a Kingfisher spotter plane was launched from the USS *Maryland* to observe the impending naval bombardment, but the flash from the ship's catapult alerted the Japanese who opened fire with the two 8in guns on the south-western end of Betio (Temakin Point), their first salvo landing 500 yards over the *Maryland*. Fire was returned by 16in shells from the battleships, heralding the start of the initial bombardment by all naval gunfire support. Unfortunately the first salvo of 16in shells from the *Maryland* knocked out all the communications radios, caused lights to go out and resulted in loss of contact with the assault formations, the *Maryland* having been chosen as communications centre for the operation.

The bombardment continued while Marines clambered down cargo nets and into LCVPs and LVTs. By 05.30 it became apparent that, due to a strong southerly current, the troop transports were out of position and were drifting into range of the Japanese batteries. The bombardment was lifted, allowing the transports to move out of range of the Japanese guns, closely followed by a flotilla of landing craft 'like ducklings following their mother', as one observer put it. The lifting of the bombardment was a golden opportunity for Admiral Shibasaki. Convinced now that the attack was coming from the north (not from the south where the Japanese themselves had landed), Shibasaki took the opportunity of transferring as many guns and men from positions in the south to bolster the positions now facing an imminent landing. Shibasaki was also happy that the attack was coming from the lagoon side, knowing full well that the landing craft would not get over the barrier reef and the Marines would have to wade 700 yards or more to the beach under murderous fire. However, he had not previously encountered Amtracs (amphibious tracked landing vehicles).

At 05.50, carrier aircraft were scheduled to arrive overhead but they were late, giving Shibasaki yet more time to prepare for the assault. When they finally arrived, the carrier aircraft – Hellcats, Avengers and Dauntless bombers – raked the island from end to end for seven minutes. Shortly after 06.00 the minesweepers *Pursuit* and *Requisite* began to clear the entrance to the lagoon, completing their work despite heavy fire from Japanese shore batteries. The entrance now clear, this enabled the destroyers USS *Ringgold* and USS *Dashiell* to enter the lagoon to engage with the shore batteries; the *Ringgold* was struck twice by 7in shells that failed to explode. The minesweeper *Pursuit* took up position on the 'line of departure' as a guide for the landing craft, switching on her searchlight for the landing craft to register.

At 07.35 the main bombardment got under way, all available guns opened up on the island and the Marines in their landing craft could easily be forgiven for thinking that nothing could still be alive on the island, but in fact most of the ships' guns were too close in and firing on a trajectory that was too flat, the shells bouncing harmlessly off the island into the sea south of Betio. The landing craft were making slow progress and there was no other option but to put H-Hour – the time the Marines would land on the beaches – back from 08.30 to 09.00. At 09.00 the bombardment was stopped, even though the landing craft were still ten minutes away. The 2nd Division Commander Julian Smith and his chief of staff, Merritt Edson, protested vigorously to Admiral Hill, but to no avail. This gave Admiral Shibasaki yet more time to prepare his defences.

The first three waves of landing craft were amphibious tractors (Amtracs), forty-two LVT-1s carrying eighteen men in each and forty-five LVT-2s carrying twenty men in each. As the first wave of Amtracs approached the reef, the Japanese defenders looked on in disbelief as these 'little swimming tanks' climbed over the reef and continued to the beaches. Behind the three lines of Amtracs were three lines of LCVPs, Higgins boats named after their designer. None of these landing craft were able to cross the reef and would have to wait for returning Amtracs to shuttle the troops to the beach, otherwise the Marines on board would face a daunting 700-yard wade under heavy fire from the lagoon reef to the beaches.

Ahead of the three waves of Amtracs, a lone LCVP was seen heading for the 700-yard-long wooden pier, which jutted out from the beach to the barrier reef. On board the LCVP was a team of Marine scout snipers led by Lieutenant William Deane Hawkins. Their job was to clear the pier and Red Beach 3 to the left. When the LCVP reached the pier, Lieutenant Hawkins, along with Second Lieutenant Leslie and four scouts, climbed onto the pier and, despite heavy Japanese small-arms fire, worked their way down the pier eliminating Japanese as they went. Second Lieutenant Leslie was carrying a flame-thrower and while clearing out a number of wooden shacks on the pier he inadvertently set the pier alight, creating a gap that would later be a hindrance to Marines offloading supplies.

Red Beach 1 was the objective of the 3rd Battalion, 2nd Marines (3/2). (Marine regiments are always referred to as 'Marines', hence 2nd Marines.) Red Beach 1 consisted almost entirely of a deep cove with numerous Japanese emplacements which took the first wave of Amtracs under murderous fire from both flanks. Several of the Amtracs were hit and others were forced over to the western side of Red Beach 1. 3/2 Marines took cover wherever they could; there was no sea wall on Red 1, unlike Red Beaches 2 and 3.

Among the men forced over to the western side of Red 1 was L Company, commanded by Major Mike Ryan. He had waded ashore from his Higgins boat stranded on the reef and, on arrival at the beach and assessing the situation, took command on the beach while awaiting the arrival of the battalion commander, Major John Schoettel, who was still held up on the reef.

Red Beach 2, which stretched from the cove of Red 1 to the west side of the long pier, was the objective of Lieutenant Colonel Herbert Amey's 2nd Battalion, 2nd Marines (2/2). Red 2 had a long sea wall running its full width; this was studded with machine-gun and rifle pits which took the front waves of Amtracs under heavy fire. None of the following waves that were in Higgins boats could get over the barrier reef and few Amtracs were returning from the beach, so the men were faced with no other alternative but to climb out of the Higgins boats and wade to shore under murderous machine-gun fire (reminiscent of the First World War). Lieutenant Colonel Amey, commander of 2/2, had commandeered an Amtrac and was heading into the beachhead when the Amtrac became entangled in a barbed-wire barricade. Unable to move, Amey and his HQ staff went over the side to wade the last 200 yards to the beach. The gunfire was so intense that they had to take cover alongside the stranded Amtrac and wait for a lull in the hail of Japanese fire coming from the sea wall. Sensing an easing of the fire, Amey and his staff headed for the beach on hands and knees, presenting as small a target as possible. Amey stood up and, shouting 'Come on, these bastards can't stop us', headed for the beach. As he stood he was hit by machine-gun fire and fell, dead, into the shallow water. Part of Amey's HQ group was Lieutenant Colonel Walter Jordan, officially an observer from the 4th Marine Division, but as the senior officer present he assumed command of 2/2. All along Red 2 casualties were severe; those Marines who made it to the sea wall went over in small groups, taking out Japanese positions, and worked their way inland, but there was little respite from the Japanese fire into the Marines wading in from the reef.

Red Beach 3 was the objective of the 2nd Battalion, 8th Marines (2/8), under Major Henry P. (Jim) Crowe. The destroyers *Ringgold* and *Dashiell* had worked their way into the lagoon and maintained a constant barrage of 5in shells onto the Japanese position on Red Beach 3, which stretched from the long pier on the right and the Burns Philp pier on the left. This enabled Crowe and his men to reach the sea wall in comparative safety (compared to Red 1 and Red 2). Crowe was the only battalion commander to reach the shore on D-Day; Schoettel was still hung up on the barrier reef of Red 1 and Amey was dead. Two Amtracs found a gap in the sea wall and advanced to the centre of the airstrip; there they took up defensive positions but soon realized they were in danger of being surrounded so they returned to the beach. All along the three beachheads (there was a substantial gap between Red 1 and Red 2), as the day went on the Marines were fearful of the possibility of a night-time counter-attack by the Japanese.

Around mid-morning 2nd Marines' Commanding Officer Colonel Shoup, who had planned the whole operation, managed to get onto Red Beach 2 after an eventful trip with his staff, first in a Higgins boat, then transferring to an Amtrac which broke down. They had to transfer to another Amtrac, eventually landing on Red 2, Shoup having received shrapnel wounds to his leg while sprinting across the beach to the sea wall. Waving away medical help, Shoup set up his command post at the side of a large Japanese bunker (which still had live Japanese inside). Shoup would remain on the island for the duration of the battle, using a captured Japanese bicycle as a crutch. With his command post established, Shoup attempted to get assessments of all three beachheads but radio communications were poor at best; however, Shoup slowly gained sufficient feedback to report to General Julian Smith on the USS *Maryland*. Shoup had contacted Major Schoettel, advising him to land on Red 2 and work west. Schoettel's reply confused Shoup: 'We have nothing left to land.' Schoettel was not aware that Major Ryan had rallied the troops on Red 1 and was working his way down Green Beach. Later Schoettel again contacted Shoup, telling him he had lost contact with his troops. Before Shoup could reply, General Julian Smith on the *Maryland* interjected, ordering Schoettel: 'Land at any cost, regain control of your battalion and continue the attack.'

Shoup instructed the 1st Battalion, 2nd Marines' Major Wood Kyle to land on Red 2 and work west, but they received such severe fire from a series of Japanese bunkers on the edge of Red 1/Red 2 that most of the Amtracs veered off to the west, landing on the west end of Red 1 where they were recruited by Major Ryan.

Around mid-morning, General Julian Smith ordered the 3rd Battalion, 8th Marines under Major Robert Ruud, who were still on board their transports, to be boated and proceed to the line of departure to be available to Colonel Shoup if needed. Prior to midday, Shoup directed Major Ruud to land on Red 3 and support Major Crowe, but no Amtracs were available. This left Ruud and his men to wade 700 yards through shallow water against murderous fire from numerous Japanese emplacements, both to their front on Red 3 and from Japanese positions to the east end of the island. Crowe's men on Red 3 could only watch in horror as their fellow Marines waded in, falling by the hundreds. Ruud ordered the fourth wave to return to boats, and shortly afterwards the 8th Marines Regimental Commander, Colonel Hall, ordered 'Land no more troops.'

General Julian Smith ordered his last reserve 1st Battalion, 8th Marines – Major Lawrence Hays – to the line of departure to await direction. Julian Smith contacted V Corps Commander General H.M. Smith for release of the 6th Marines to him as a reserve. This request was granted at around 14.30 when Julian Smith radioed Shoup that the 1/8 was at the line of departure awaiting Shoup's directive to land. This message never got through to Shoup, so Smith ordered Hays to land on the extreme east of the island, work north-west and link up with Shoup on Red 2. Hays also never got this message, so 1/8 spent the rest of D-Day and the night in their landing craft.

On Red Beach 1, Major Ryan was able to contact Shoup, informing him that he was intending to advance along Green Beach as Red 1 was still under heavy fire from the cluster of strongpoints at the junction between Red Beach 1 and 2. Ryan had moderate success in advancing along Green Beach, taking by flanking fire Japanese positions that were set to face out to sea. As the afternoon wore on, Ryan decided to pull his line of attack back to make a defensive line, ready for the Japanese counter-attack which he, like all the other Marines on Betio, expected to come after dark.

The 75mm Pack Howitzers of 1/10 – Lieutenant Colonel Rixey – were still boated and hung up on the reef off Red 2. It was after dark that 1/10's howitzers could be landed, but they were ready for work on the morning of D+1. M4-A2 medium (Sherman) tanks had spent most of D-Day trying to get ashore. Eight Shermans headed into Red 3; one flooded out but the remaining seven made it to land and Major Crowe sent them east to support him with advancing infantry. On Red 1, only two of six Shermans made it to land. These two tanks moved inland and tied up with Major Ryan advancing along Green Beach. In the afternoon an incident on Red 3 almost certainly changed the outcome of the battle in the Marines' favour. A naval artillery spotter with Major Crowe observed a group of what appeared to be Japanese officers with two tanks in the open by a large reinforced concrete bunker. Fearing a counter-attack led by tanks, the observer contacted the destroyers *Ringgold* and *Dashiell* for a 5in salvo fused for air-burst on the group. *Ringgold* and *Dashiell* were right on target: one tank was disabled, the other retired and the group of officers was wiped out to a man. The salvo had wiped out Admiral Shibasaki and his whole staff, who were attempting to move their HQ south, away from the front line of Marines on Red 3. Shibasaki would have undoubtedly ordered a night-time counter-attack, but with the admiral dead and without inter-unit communication, all the Japanese units were left to fend for themselves, defending their individual positions to the death.

At dawn on D+1 Marines all over Betio wondered what had happened to the expected counter-attack, not being aware that Shibasaki was dead. He would most likely have ordered an all-out counter-attack overnight. The situation on the beaches was far from ideal; there was a 600-yard gap between Major Ryan and his motley band on Red 1/Green Beach and the Marines on Red 2 and the extreme left of Red 1. Major Crowe on Red 3 had advanced inland and to the east and was tied in with Red 2 at the long pier.

Major Hays' 1/8 was still in Higgins boats at the line of departure; they had been there for nearly twenty-four hours. At 06.15 Hays was ordered to land on Red 2 but his Higgins boats still could not get over the barrier reef, so they were faced with a 600-yard wade through the lagoon in the face of heavy Japanese machine-gun and rifle fire coming from not only beachfront Japanese emplacements but also from two machine guns sited in the *Saidu Maru*, a cargo ship that had run aground on the barrier reef earlier in the year (this ship is often mistakenly identified as the *Niminoa*, a wooden inter-island steamer that the British captain had run aground on the reef prior to the arrival of the Japanese on Tarawa). Hays' 1/8 suffered 50 per cent casualties wading to shore on Red 2.

Shoup called a temporary halt to Hays' men while aircraft bombed and strafed the *Saidu Maru* but it was only silenced by gunfire from the USS *Maryland* and *Colorado*. Shoup was determined to get men across the island to the south side, thus cutting the Japanese defence in two. He already had men dug in in the airstrip's internal triangle, but they were virtually trapped in by Japanese machine guns sited at either end of the airstrip. Following a concentrated air strike from carrier planes, men – mostly from 1/2 on Red 2 – raced across the open ground of the airstrip, reached the south beaches and dug in. The Japanese counter-attacked in the afternoon from the east, but were beaten back by the Marines in spite of heavy casualties. Later in the afternoon Shoup sent Colonel Jordan and his 2/2 command over to the south shore to take command. Jordan radioed Shoup to inform him that he only had around 200 men including thirty wounded, and was low on ammunition, food and water. Shoup ordered Jordan to hold and await re-supply.

On Red 3 Major Crowe's 2/8, along with the remains of Major Ruud's 3/8 that had been attached to Crowe, continued to try to advance inland and to the east, but were held up by a complex of bunkers just beyond the Burns Philp pier, much to the annoyance of Jim Crowe.

The biggest success of D+1 was with Mike Ryan and his men on Green Beach, bolstered by the arrival of two Sherman tanks ('China Gal' and 'Cecilia') and following bombardment from two destroyers all along Green Beach. Following the bombardment, Ryan and his men with his two tanks swept down Green Beach, reaching the two 8in Vickers gun emplacements at Temakin Point on the south-west corner of Betio by 1100 hours. Ryan prepared to re-group and advance east along Red 1 but was ordered by Shoup to deploy in defence of Green Beach, which was now entirely in Marine hands. By 16.00 the situation was much improved, allowing Shoup to radio General Julian Smith a detailed assessment, ending with 'casualties many, percentage dead unknown, combat efficiency – WE ARE WINNING.'

On the evening of D+1, Colonel Edson, Divisional Chief of Staff, arrived to take over from the almost exhausted Colonel Shoup. Edson sent Shoup first to get his now-infected leg wounds tended to, followed by some much-needed sleep. Shoup would remain as Edson's assistant for the duration of the battle. During the night of D+1/D+2 Edson and the newly-treated and rested Shoup planned the following day's attack.

The plan of attack was to advance on three fronts. Jones's 1/6 was to pass through Major Ryan's 1/2 and 2/2 entrenched on the southern shore (Black Beach). Major Hays' 1/8 was to move west from Red 2 and assault the large pocket of emplacements at the junction of Red 1 and Red 2, which had wreaked havoc since D-Day. Both 2/8 and 3/8 were to advance eastwards from the Burns Philp pier on Red 3. Lieutenant Colonel McLeod's 3/6, who had been boated at the line of departure since 16.00 on D+1, finally landed on Green Beach. Experiencing light resistance, Jones's 1/6 reached the entrenched 1/2, 2/2 by 11.00 and after a brief rest continued to attack eastwards on the narrowing tail end of Betio.

On Red 2, Hays' 1/8 began their assault on the Red 1/Red 2 stronghold, but made little headway despite the assistance of tanks and two SPMs (Self-Propelled Mounts), 75mm guns mounted on half-tracks. By the end of D+2 the 'pocket', as it became known to the Marines, was still very much intact.

Jim Crowe's composite 2/8, 3/8 advanced eastwards but were held up by a collection of three major emplacements – a steel pillbox, a coconut-log and sand machine-gun emplacement and a large concrete sand-covered shelter – all mutually supporting. A lucky mortar round from the Marines landed in the ammunition dump of the log and sand emplacement, causing the whole dump and emplacement to blow apart in spectacular fashion. Engineers with TNT satchel charges and the support of a Sherman tank were able to eliminate the steel pillbox. The concrete and sand-covered emplacement held out for over an hour, but finally engineers with demolition charges and flame-throwers, led by Lieutenant Alexander 'Sandy' Bonnyman, secured the top of the emplacement and began to drop hand grenades down the vertical ventilator pipes, flushing out more than 200 Japanese who tried to dislodge the Marines from the top. Most of the Japanese were hit by canister shot from supporting M3 Stuart tanks; those who made it to the top were dispatched by Bonnyman and his 'forlorn hope'. The Marines held the top of the emplacement, but Lieutenant Bonnyman was killed in the defence. He was later to be awarded a posthumous Medal of Honor.

With the obstacles cleared, Crowe's 2/8 and 3/8 were able to advance and tie in with Jones's left flank at the east end of the airstrip. With the exception of the 'pocket', all objectives for D+2 had been accomplished. General Julian Smith landed on Green Beach mid-morning and, after touring the Marine-held western section of the island, joined Edson and Shoup at Shoup's CP on Red 2. There was, however, plenty of fight left in the Japanese. On Jones's 1/6 front, at 19.30 fifty Rikusentai started probing 1/6's front. A brief but bloody hand-to-hand fight ensued, but after one hour the Japanese retired. At 03.00 a much larger attack by several hundred Japanese, charging and shouting 'Marines, you die!' occurred to the battalion's front. Naval gunfire was called in on the east end of Betio and Marine artillery was called in as close as 50 yards in front of Jones's men. Dawn revealed more than 200 dead Japanese in front of the Marine lines, with a further 125 mangled bodies lying further east, victims of the naval gunfire. Jones's 1/6 had suffered 45 dead and 138 wounded.

On the morning of 23 November, D-Day + 3, McLeod's 3/6 passed through Jones's 1/6, exhausted by the previous Banzai charge, the ground littered with the carnage of the hand-to-hand fighting. McLeod's Marines pressed on ahead with the assistance of two medium Sherman and seven M3 Stuart light tanks. Progress was good until they reached the eastern anti-tank ditch just east of the airstrip. On the east side of the anti-tank ditch were a series of trenches and pillboxes. To maintain momentum, McLeod bypassed the strongpoint, leaving L Company and three tanks to reduce it. After a hard fight the blockhouse and trenches were subdued, the Marines counting 475 Japanese dead for 9 dead and 25 wounded of their own. McLeod's men reached the extreme east end of Betio at 1300 hours. The whole of Betio was now in Marine hands, with the exception of the 'pocket' on Red 1/2, which still held out after three days of the Marines' attempts to take it.

To deal with the pocket once and for all, Shoup planned to surround it around the back (south) side (the bulk of the Japanese weapons were pointing seaward (north)). Shoup planned for Hays' 1/8 to attack from the east (Red 2) with flame-throwers and demolition charges. At the same time, Schoettel's 3/2 would move from their area west of the airstrip to join up with Hays' 1/8. Hays sent two SPMs and a platoon of infantry out onto the reef to complete the encirclement of the pocket. With fire from the SPMs' 75mm guns pounding the front of the pocket and engineers with flame-throwers and satchel charges assaulting the other three sides, the pocket finally fell. Hays' and Schoettel's men joined at the airstrip's north revetments, taking the pocket from the rear. This finished resistance from the pocket; a few Japanese troops tried to escape but were mown down by the Marines. A small number surrendered and others committed suicide inside the ruins of the pocket. At 1300 hours Colonel Shoup advised General Julian Smith that the pocket had fallen and enemy opposition had collapsed; the island was now in Marine hands (although there were still Japanese holed up all over the island and it would take days of mopping up). At noon on 24 November, General Julian Smith, along with General Holland Smith who had arrived from Makin Island, witnessed the ceremonial raising of the Stars and Stripes. Also raised was the British Union flag, signifying the return of British rule to the Gilbert Islands.

Ralph Butler was a member of K Company, 3rd Battalion, 2nd Marines and took part in the battle for Tarawa for the full seventy-six hours. He returned to Betio with the author of this book in 1993 for the fiftieth anniversary, the first time since the battle took place. The following is an account of Ralph's memories of those terrible seventy-six hours, typical of many Marines who fought there:

As the trip to Tarawa draws nearer, I'm wondering what it is that's drawing me back after fifty years. The memories vary. Some remain stark and graphic, others are just bits and pieces, fragmented like some dreams. For the past couple of years I've been in touch with a couple of buddies who were on the beach with me as members of K-3-2. As we write back and forth we remind one another of incidents that individually we were vague about and now, as I am preparing to go back, I'm making an effort to recall things as they happened for me fifty years ago.

We, the twenty-sixth replacement Bn, arrived in Wellington, New Zealand just as the division was in the process of embarking and loading troop transports, though we didn't get to see much of New Zealand; what we did see left me with wanting to see much more.

Hiv Cable, Ed Ezzell and I were assigned K-3-2 and while aboard the *Arthur Middleton* I was assigned to Cpl Dommel's machine-gun squad as an ammo carrier. I believe Hiv and Easy were in the 60 mortars at the time. Among the Marines I remember from the machine-gun section at the time were Tommy Sparr, Frank Mumford (who had his helmet hit by a bullet which went in and out and just grazed Frank's head), Jones, Taylor and Horwitz.

In any case, the squad I was assigned to went in the first wave of Amtracs and as I remember I thought we had about fourteen men in the Amtrac, but others say they held more than that. Our Amtrac was hit hard and often going in, which was quite a shock because we were led to believe there would be very few Japs left alive to offer any resistance. After a very turbulent and explosive ride we ground to a halt and those of us able leapt out; the time was about 09.00. As far as I remember the Amtrac never moved after it stopped.

The part of the beach (Red Beach 1) where we landed was wide open, there was no sea wall. Already there were dead Marines and we rushed for shell holes, anything for protection. Trying to remember names at the unprotected pocket of beach I come up with these: Dommel, Jones, Taylor, Ezzell, Cable, Van Buskirk. I was in a hole with Gunny Van Buskirk who was wounded at the time, as were most of the men who weren't already dead. I remember a blond Marine who was running down the beach, his helmet off and blood spurting out of his throat and before anyone could get to him he was riddled to pieces.

I recognized two of my buddies from the twenty-sixth replacements among the bodies on the beach and that, along with the horrific fire and shell coming from all sides, suddenly made me realize that this was a very bad situation.

All the men in that pocket were brave gutsy guys, but Gunny Van Buskirk was exceptionally great in my opinion. He was cool, calm and collected and he impressed me greatly. I wonder whatever happened to him for I never saw him after the first day.

I think it was about noon or after that Gunny Van Buskirk asked me to run down towards the tip of the island and see if I could get a hold of 'Baker' Co and tell them of our situation, not knowing of course that everyone was in the same boat. I did get further down the beach but, as I remember it, the only one I came across was a Marine from either 'I' or 'L' Company. I remember as night fell there was just us two surrounded by dead Marines and Japs and we were huddled in a hole next to a crippled Amtrac. We spent a futile amount of time trying to disassemble the Amtrac's machine guns to have in the hole with us, as we were dead certain it was our last night on earth. I remember we had a little spat about movements of people silhouetted by fire to our west; I thought they were Japs, he thought they were Marines. On closer look I decided he was right and concentrated on the front. He got upset, and rightly so, for I didn't tell him that he was right. But we got through the night and in the morning we each tried to get back to our own companies. I know he made it through Tarawa OK, for we saw each other in Hawaii and I sure hope he made it through the rest of the war. I wish I could remember his name for he was a good Marine and I hope he has a good life.

Like I say, things come back to me patchwork-like. I think it was the second I hooked up with a Marine named Horwitz who was in my machine-gun section. I remember we had a light .30 with ammo and Horwitz used me as his assistant gunner. We set up at pillboxes near the pier. We emptied the belt into the slits in the boxes, guided by the tracers. I liked Horwitz, he was a fiery guy and another one I would like to get in touch with if God willing he's still living.

I can't remember sleeping during the entire time on Tarawa. I think it was the third day when we reached the airstrip. Ed Ezzell, who had one of the biggest amount of Japs killed that I know of on the island, was trying to start an old Jap truck. Cable and the rest of us were ducking for cover in case it was booby-trapped. He got it started, but there was nowhere he could go with it; it wasn't exactly the Autobahn there. It must have been the third day also when I was helping pull wounded out of the section where we first landed.

Water was scarce, the canteens we brought with us were long gone and the 5 gal cans that made it ashore were rancid. All of our lips were swollen like saucers and split.

I remember when we were on the other side of the island, I forget which day it was, Frank Mumford, Tommy Sparr, Joe Bonotiglio and myself stripped and went into the ocean to rinse off and cool off, figuring things had quieted down enough to do so. A couple of dismembered bodies floated by us and by this time we were immune to shock. The stench was something no-one who was there will ever forget. It was overwhelming. It penetrated your pores and it seemed like it took weeks after to rid your body of it, real or imagined I don't know. Years later, as an elevator mechanic, I had occasion to service elevators in the slaughterhouses in Cleveland and though the odors were terrible they couldn't compare with the stench on Betio.

I would love to get in touch with all of the Marines I named plus all the guys who were with us. As a kid who celebrated his eighteenth birthday aboard the *Arthur Middleton* en route to Tarawa it was an experience I will never forget. The acts of heroism and bravery and perseverance I witnessed in those four days will always remain with me.

PFC Ralph G. Butler

K-3-2

Although Betio was now in US Marine hands, there was still work to be done. There remained several days of clearing Betio of any Japanese hidden on the island. The 2nd Marine Division still had three tasks outstanding:

1. Securing the rest of Tarawa Atoll.
2. The capture of Apamama Atoll (known to have a Japanese garrison in place), and
3. The capture of Abaiang, Marakei and Maiana atolls.

The job of securing the rest of Tarawa Atoll was given to Lieutenant Colonel Murray's 2nd Battalion, 6th Marines. The 2/6 had seen the least action during the assault on Betio and began their task early in the morning of 24 November by transferring from Betio to Buota at the east of Tarawa Atoll. During the fight for Betio, a considerable number of Rikusentai had been observed crossing over from Betio to Bairiki Island and disappearing up the other islands of the atoll.

Before Murray's 2/6 commenced their work, some reconnaissance had already been carried out. On 21 November, while the battle for Betio raged, Company D, 2nd Tank Battalion (Scout Company) under Captain John Nelson landed on Eita, Buota and several other unnamed locations. On the same day the 3rd Platoon landed on Eita, where it found fuel dumps, bomb and mine dumps, but no Japanese. The 2nd Platoon landed on Buota, the islet that makes the bend at the elbow of the atoll, and located a Japanese position estimated to contain 100 of the enemy, and a radio station at the corner of the bend. The 1st Platoon landed about 4 miles further up the atoll to the north-west, near Tabiteuea village, where it captured one Japanese labourer and several islanders.

The 3rd Battalion, 10th Marines, was sent to Eita on 23 November and the 3rd Platoon, Company D, was attached to the artillery battalion. The platoon had captured one Japanese prisoner. Just after dark on the same day the Japanese force on Buota moved north through the positions of the 1st Platoon, Company D. Next day, the 1st and 4th platoons scouted as far north as the island called Ida, about halfway up the long side of the atoll. In the meantime, Nelson met the 2nd Battalion, 6th Marines, on Buota and guided the battalion as far north as Julia. On the following day the scouts were recalled to Eita to prepare for reconnaissance missions on the atolls adjacent to Tarawa; these being Abaiang, Marakei and Maiana. Murray's battalion embarked in boats from Betio at 05.00 on 24 November and moved over to Buota to begin the trek to the north. By nightfall the battalion had advanced to Buoti, (not to be confused with Buota, which is a separate island), passing through several islander villages which had recently been evacuated. No enemy force was encountered.

The march was resumed on 25 November and at the end of the day the battalion was well up the atoll. Still no contact with the enemy had been made and by late afternoon of 26 November the 2nd Battalion, 6th Marines had reached the south end of the last large island at the north-west end of Tarawa Atoll, named Buariki. Before bivouacking for the night, Murray sent out Company E to the north-west to maintain a position as an advance covering force. Murray knew from information he had received from the scouts that somewhere north of him were at least a hundred Japanese. The enemy group had to be on Buariki. This was verified when patrols from Company E ran into a Japanese patrol at sunset. A brief fire-fight ensued, in which two Marines were wounded and it was believed that two or three Japanese were killed. After dark, Company E's patrols returned and the company remained in its defensive position during the night. Occasional harassing enemy rifle fire was received, but the Marines held their fire and waited for daylight. There were no further Marine casualties.

Next morning, Murray advanced with two companies in assault and one in reserve to clear the area between his position of the night before and the place where the island narrows, north-east of Buariki village. Shortly after moving out, the companies found the enemy position. Although the Japanese had no organized line, it was difficult to destroy them. Broken into small groups, each one in a pit or behind coconut logs, the enemy held their fire until the Marines were almost on top of them. Vegetation was dense and the fighting was at close range. Company E was hit hard and paused to reorganize themselves. Murray then moved Company F through Company E to continue the attack. In the meantime, Company G was coming in on the enemy's east flank, attacking to the north-west. Murray had with him one artillery battery, Battery G, 10th Marines, but the action was at such close range that it made it impossible to use the howitzers, except for one concentration that was fired when Company F passed through Company E.

After several hours of typical jungle fighting, the main enemy resistance was overcome and Murray turned his attention to mopping up and patrolling. The day's action cost 3 officers killed and 1 wounded; enlisted losses were 29 killed and 58 wounded. Some 175 Japanese were killed and 2 Korean labourers captured.

One tiny islet, Naa or Lone Tree islet, was still to be taken. This islet lay a hundred yards north-west of Buariki. Early on the morning of 28 November Murray sent troops over to Naa, which was found to have no Japanese, and by 08.00 the capture of Tarawa Atoll was complete. The 2nd Battalion, 6th Marines then returned to Eita to rest and reorganize after the long march up the atoll.

Apamama

On 22 October 1943, Major General Holland M. Smith, commanding the 5th Amphibious Corps, ordered Captain James L. Jones, commanding the 5th Amphibious Corps Reconnaissance Company, to land his company, minus one platoon, on Apamama during the night of 19/20 November, with a mission to reconnoitre the atoll in order to determine whether there was any Japanese force ashore and to select and mark suitable beaches and channels to be used later by other forces. If any large hostile force was found to be present on Apamama, Jones was to withdraw and avoid an engagement. Jones's company was to be lifted to Apamama on the submarine *Nautilus*, the same *Nautilus* that had taken Carlson's Raiders to Makin Island in August 1942.

Apamama Atoll (also called Hopper Atoll, Abemama and Apemama) lies 76 miles south of Tarawa. Being elliptical in shape, its lagoon is almost entirely enclosed by Abemama Island, a long island broken in five places, so that it appears there are six islands closely joined together. Across the south-western side of the atoll there is a reef through which there are two passages suitable for small ships. The south-western side of the atoll is guarded by two islands separate from Abemama, named Abatiku and Entrance Islands. To avoid confusion, the six portions of Abemama were given code names, as were the islands of Tarawa Atoll. The north segment was named

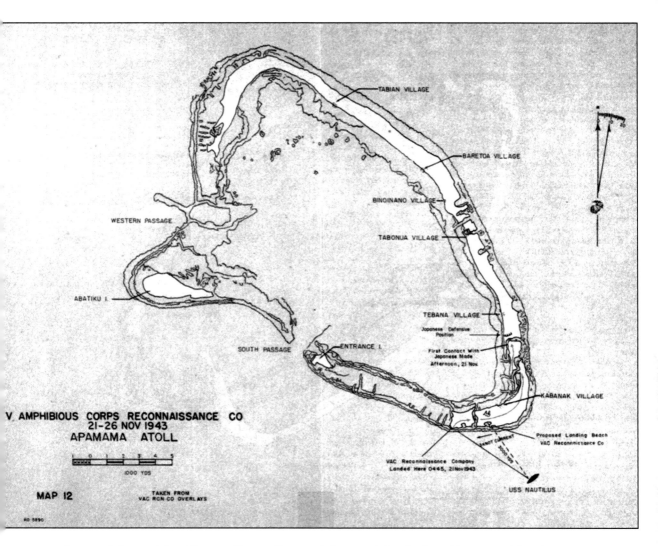

V AMPHIBIOUS CORPS RECONNAISSANCE CO
21-26 NOV 1943
APAMAMA ATOLL

MAP 12

TAKEN FROM
VAC RCN CO OVERLAYS

Steve, followed by Oscar, Otto, Orson, John and finally Joe. Entrance Island was named Nick and Abatiku was Matt. The whole atoll is about 12 miles long and 5 miles wide and is surrounded by a continuous reef, broken only by the South Passage and Western Passage. Inside the lagoon there is a considerable amount of foul ground and coral heads. Coconut palms and tropical vegetation can be found in abundance on all the islands of the atoll.

In addition to her role of carrying corps scouts to Apamama, *Nautilus* had another mission to be completed first. From Pearl Harbor the ship was to go to Tarawa, cruise in that area prior to the landing on Betio to observe Japanese movements and positions and be available to rescue pilots of the attacking planes if they were shot down during the pre-D-Day softening-up process. *Nautilus* was then to leave Tarawa on 19 November in order to land the scouts on Apamama. The submarine, with the corps scouts on board, carried out her first mission off Betio according to plan. In the afternoon of 19 November, *Nautilus* left Betio for Apamama. A strong current held to a minimum the pace of the submerged craft, which was at best a slow ship. Shortly after 19.30 she surfaced and began to make better time. Shortly after 21.00 on 19 November a destroyer from Task Force 53, now approaching Tarawa, opened fire on *Nautilus* under the impression that she was an enemy craft and scored a direct hit on the main induction tube with a 5in shell. After she had dived to a depth of about 300ft, emergency measures were taken to right the ship and several hours later she was able to re-surface and carry out temporary repairs to the damage. All next day she had to remain submerged and arrived off Apamama at approximately 14.00. After sundown a run was made to the south to give an opportunity to charge her batteries; she then returned to Apamama to discharge the corps scouts in their rubber boats.

Long before dawn on the morning of 21 November Jones's company left the submarine and headed towards John Island. The boats drifted off course in a strong current and they landed on Joe instead of John. Once ashore, the scouts began patrolling and had one minor brush with the enemy when a three-man patrol was encountered. One Japanese was killed. The company then moved to the next islet, Orson. Here islanders reported that there were twenty-five Japanese on Apamama and their positions were just across from the north end of Orson on the south end of Otto. Attempts to cross the sandspit connecting Orson and Otto were unsuccessful; the Japanese, being strongly entrenched in fortified positions, laid down heavy fire from light machine guns and rifles. As it was already late in the day, Jones broke off the action and withdrew to plan for the next day's attack. It appeared that without mortars it would be impossible to dislodge the Japanese from their positions.

On the morning of 24 November, Jones moved his platoons to the north end of Orson and called in seventy rounds of fire from *Nautilus* on the Japanese positions. The enemy continued to fire while the submarine was firing and Jones was unable to use rubber boats to outflank the Japanese. Late in the day, a destroyer offered her services and fired a few rounds as it grew dark. Next morning an islander arrived at Jones's camp with the news that the Japanese were all dead. This information was corroborated by another islander who had given reliable information before. The 1st and 3rd platoons were sent to investigate and found the story to be true. A few of the enemy had been killed by the shelling and the remainder, around eighteen, had committed hara-kiri (ritual suicide).

The following morning a landing force commanded by Brigadier General Leo D. Hermle arrived to occupy Apamama. With the arrival of the 3rd Battalion, 6th Marines, Jones received orders to embark his company aboard the *Harris* and depart the atoll. The 5th Amphibious Corps scouts had lost few men; one being killed in action, one wounded in action and one injured. The enemy loss was absolute, with twenty-three dead.

Apamama: 2nd Marine Division

On 24 November 1943, General Julian C. Smith directed Brigadier General Hermle to seize and occupy Apamama atoll. Hermle was to be in charge of a landing force built around the 3rd Battalion, 6th Marines, commanded by Lieutenant Colonel K.F. McLeod. Hermle was instructed that the 5th Amphibious Corps Reconnaissance Company had secured two islands of the atoll and that there were about twenty-five Japanese holding out from fortified positions. Rear Admiral Harry Hill was to provide the naval task force necessary to lift Hermle's landing force to Apamama. At 15.00 on 25 November, General Hermle, aboard the *Maryland* with Admiral Hill and the 3rd Battalion, 6th Marines on the *Harris* left for Apamama. During the uneventful voyage to the target, Admiral Hill received word from corps scouts that all the Japanese on Apamama were dead. Next morning, the force arrived at Apamama and Lieutenant Colonel McLeod sent two of his rifle companies ashore: Company I on John Island and Company K on Steve Island. General Hermle went ashore on the morning of the same day to organize the atoll's defences and arrange a meeting with native chiefs and acquaint them with his plans for occupying the atoll.

On 1 December, General Julian C. Smith arrived to inspect the progress of unloading supplies and equipment and the atoll's defences. In the meantime, the 8th Defence Battalion had arrived and had emplaced their weapons. The air base commander was also ashore. On 4 December, General Hermle received orders from Admiral Hill to pass the command of Apamama Atoll to the base commander, Captain W.P. Cogswell, USN. Hermle left the atoll that same day to rejoin the division.

The Abaiang, Marakei and Maiana Atolls

On 29 November, Company D, 2nd Tank Battalion embarked aboard the minesweeper *Pursuit* with the mission of reconnoitring three island atolls adjacent to Tarawa: Abaiang, Marakei and Maiana. There was a possibility that Japanese coastwatchers might still be on these islands. Before dawn on 30 November, Company D landed two rubber boatloads of men, above and below the village of Koinawa in Abaiang Atoll. Five Japanese on the island left immediately in a native boat and were last seen sailing across the lagoon. Islanders were contacted ashore and arrangements were made with them to take care of the Japanese if they should return. The next atoll to be reconnoitred was Marakei. Here the *Pursuit* was greeted by several boats filled with islanders, who supplied information that there were no Japanese on the atoll. In order to confirm this, four boatloads of scouts went ashore and found that there were indeed no Japanese. After leaving food and medical supplies for the islanders, the *Pursuit* turned back to Abaiang to pick up the scouts who had landed there earlier in the day and had been prevented by bad weather from being taken off sooner.

The next morning, 1 December, the scouts landed on Maiana, near the village of Bickerel. No Japanese were present on Maiana and after a brief reconnaissance the scouts returned to the *Pursuit* and were back in Tarawa lagoon by noon.

The Division leaves Tarawa

With the reconnaissance of Abaiang, Marakei and Maiana atolls complete and the arrival of defence battalions and other troops to garrison Tarawa and Apamama, the 2nd Marine Division prepared to leave the Gilberts. The 2nd and 8th Marines had left soon after the battle on Betio and were now in the division's new base camp at Kamuela, Hawaii. During the last week in November most of the remaining units of the division, except the 2nd Battalion, 6th Marines, which stayed for two more months, embarked aboard ship and sailed for Hawaii. On 4 December General Julian C. Smith turned over the command of the Tarawa area to Commander, Advanced Base, Tarawa: Captain Jackson R. Tate, USN.

The cost of capturing Tarawa raised a storm of criticism in the United States when it was learned that the casualty figures amounted to roughly 3,000 killed, wounded or missing in action. Too far removed from the realism of war, the American people were caught between shock and surprise; there was nothing to prepare them for the cost involved in making amphibious operations against a tenacious, fanatical foe who was willing to die to the last man for Emperor and Empire. For a while the hue and cry raised by the Press almost obscured the facts.

Subsequent amphibious operations in the Marianas, at Peleliu and at Iwo Jima, helped to give perspective to Tarawa, but by then the bloody violent struggle was half-forgotten. Succeeding operations did much to dim the memory of Tarawa, but none ever obscured it. Nothing could ever obscure such a battle, where perseverance dominated over adversity, where individual courage and collective know-how defeated a strong Japanese garrison on its own ground and in its own positions.

As a contemporary national magazine put it: 'Last week some 2,000 or 3,000 United States Marines, most of them now dead or wounded, gave the nation a name to stand beside those of Concord Bridge, the *Bonhomme Richard*, the Alamo, Little Big Horn and Belleau Wood. The name was Tarawa.'

The Photographers

What follows is Staff Sergeant Dick Hannah, Marine Corps combat correspondent's account of the combat cameramen's work on Betio, Tarawa. Their photos (many in colour) and movie footage would shock America, many images of dead Marines floating in the lagoon only being released after approval from President Roosevelt:

> News photographers, as everyone knows, accept danger as an inherent part of their jobs. They thrive on it. But never before had any team of cameramen been

called upon to face the terrific concentration of hazards and hardships which confronted the men behind the lenses at Tarawa. To make the beach and remain in one piece certainly was a full-time task in itself. Consider then the colossal accomplishments of Betio's photographers. Throughout the seventy-six terrifying hours, with an excellent prospect of death at every step, the men with the cameras filmed each phase of the battle as it developed. A photographer jumped from one of the first amphibious tractors that clattered ashore and there was one with the flame-throwing Marines who roasted the last Japs in their buried pillboxes.

The pictures that came out of Tarawa were acclaimed the finest and most startling records of combat ever produced. Magazine and newspaper editors were stunned by the superbness of their grim realism and stark, living action. For weeks, front pages featured the faithful reproductions of battle at its bitterest. America could see – and appreciate – what its Marines in the Pacific were up against. Newsreel audiences too could gasp as the startling films flashed across the nation's screens. They gasped – and grew more conscious of the war.

Of paramount importance, though, was that military leaders possessed a complete and graphic record of what had happened at Tarawa. The pictures, both moving and still, proved invaluable in training and planning for future operations. The majority of these films were produced by members of the photographic section attached to headquarters of the Second Marine Division. Officer in charge of that section was Captain Louis Hayward, former film star who swapped his part of Hollywood's glamour for the life of a Leatherneck on July 1, 1942. Although he had been overseas for most of his then-16 months' service, the Captain got his first taste of combat at Tarawa. There, Louis Hayward's real-life role proved vastly more daring and exciting than had been any of his swashbuckling screen portrayals (*The Count of Monte Cristo*, *The Man in the Iron Mask*, etc.).

Much of the breathtaking movie footage of Betio was shot in Kodachrome by the Captain himself. Carrying two 16mm cameras, he went in with an early wave and waged a ceaseless campaign, capturing a multiplicity of the most violent scenes ashore. To him went the unstinting praise of his superior officers for his excellent organizational work – for the glorious performance of the Marine photographers he had trained for many months and for his own spectacular contributions in film.

Following is a roster of the enlisted men who comprised the Second Division's headquarters photo section: Technical Sergeant Carlos Steele (Paulding, Ohio); Staff Sergeant Norman Hatch (Washington DC); Staff Sergeant Roy Olund (Rio Linda, California); Staff Sergeant John F. Ercole (White Plains, New York); Sergeant Forrest Owens (Bozeman, Montana); Sergeant Ferman H.

Dixon (Morganton, North Carolina); Sergeant Ernest J. Diet (Hammond, Louisiana); Corporal Obie E. Newcomb Jr. (Crestwood, New York); Corporal Jack Ely (Lowell, Washington); Corporal Raymond Katjasic (Cleveland, Ohio); Corporal Jim R. Orton (Stratford, California); Private First Class William Kelliher (Kansas City, Missouri); Private Chris C. Demo, Pontiac, Michigan

Staff Sergeant Jefferson H. Sutton, former cameraman for International News Photos in Los Angeles, California, covered operations of the Division's artillery regiment. The only two civilian photographers who went in with the early waves were Don Senick, 20th Century Fox Movietone News, and Frank Filan, Associated Press. Johnny Florea of *Time* and *Life* filmed the attack from a Navy dive bomber.

Second-in-command to Captain Hayward was Marine Gunner John F. Leopold from Wooster, Ohio, a Warrant Officer veteran of Guadalcanal. He was the first man to return to the States from Tarawa. Red-bearded and gruff-spoken, Gunner Leopold (pre-war instructor of photography at the Washington DC National Art School) re-joined the Marines the day after Pearl Harbor. He has five years' previous active service with the Corps and his record boasted four years of reserve time. Gunner Leopold hit the beach at Betio on the morning of November 21, his forty-first birth-day. Four days later, on Thanksgiving, he left the island in a four-motor Navy patrol bomber, carrying with him the precious cargo of film which was to be accorded such record-breaking reproduction. His story, told on arrival at Marine Corps Head-quarters and published in the February 1944 issue of *U.S. Camera* magazine, is repeated below:

> When we headed for Tarawa, there were fifteen men (including the Captain and myself) in our photo section. Some had been former newsmen, others never had held a camera until they joined the Marine Corps. Many of them were youngsters of 21 or 22 years. Of our 'Skipper', Captain Hayward, I know that I speak for every man in our outfit in saying that we could not have had a more capable leader or one who could command more respect.
>
> Before we left our base for the combat area, the Captain called us together and gave us a little 'pep talk' which I think was greatly responsible for the results we got at Tarawa.
>
> 'I know all of us are fed up,' he said, 'with hearing about the "marvelous" photography coming out of the European war. This time, let's really give 'em something to talk about – from the Marines in the Pacific.'
>
> And that was the idea each of us carried over the sides of the transports as we scrambled down cargo nets to our landing craft. We had split up the section to make sure photographers would be in every part of the convoy. It was the first time in the history of amphibious warfare that photographers had landed to

take a beach-head with initial assault waves. Some of us went in Higgins boats, others in tank lighters and still others in amphibious tractors.

We had among us one 3¼″ × 4¼″ and eight 4″ × 5″ Speed-Graphic news cameras. These were equipped with Anastigmat f/4.5 lenses of 127mm focal length. Film packs of Super XX film were used with all the cameras. We carried no cut film since we knew that it would be impossible to reload and because holders added too much extra weight. Only one of the cameras was equipped with a flash gun. We used midget bulbs for shooting interiors of pillboxes and dugouts after the battle. The use of flash bulbs during battle would have given away our positions.

We had seven 16mm magazine-load Cine movie cameras. With these, we shot nothing but color film. The film had not been tropical-packed, so before leaving our rear base we had dipped the boxes in wax. Apparently, from results, it was sufficient protection against the murderous heat. On most of the movie cameras, we used one- and two-inch lenses. We had others available, up to six inches, but because of unsteadiness we did not use them. Anticipating this unsteadiness (caused by the motion of the small boats, uncertain positions on shore and our own excited shaking), some of us had mounted our cameras on gun stocks similar to that of the Tommy gun. This trick proved to be quite a help.

There were three 35mm Eyemo movie cameras and one 35mm Wahl sound camera. Though it was taken ashore, the latter, because of its size, was not put to use during the landing operations. In addition, each of us had a 35mm miniature Kodak, just in case something happened to the larger equipment (two of our men were blown out of their boats. Their 4″x5″ cameras were lost in the action). With the exception of what we were using as we went ashore, most of us put our extra equipment into meteorological balloons and wired the open ends tightly. They made perfect waterproof containers. We took no darkroom equipment since the plan was to get in, make our pictures and get out. All the film was developed at Pearl Harbor and printed in Washington!

At 4 o'clock on the morning of D-Day, November 20, I got into a Higgins boat which was to land a 37mm anti-tank gun and its crew. In the same boat was Don Senick, the 20th Century Fox Movietone News man. My assistant, Sergeant Ferman H. Dixon, was with me. That was the longest, hottest day I have ever known. We made several charges toward shore, but each time the enemy fire was so heavy that we had to turn back. All day long, as we bobbed offshore beneath a blazing sun, the Japs peppered us with everything they had. Fortunately, we escaped a direct hit from the big pieces. Other boats, all around us, were blown right out of existence.

At first, my only instinct was to duck when a shell would whistle our way. Then I thought 'If they're going to hit us, it won't do any good to duck   might just as well make pictures while I can.' So, with quaking knees and pounding heart, I stood up and filmed everything I could see. I had two of the 16mm movie cameras and kept them grinding all day long. Senick, too, shot all the action from our boat. On one of our first attempts to get ashore, a very near miss from one of the big Jap guns bounced us into the air and sent shrapnel tearing through one side of our boat. Luckily, we landed right side up – with the boat still beneath us.

Night eventually came and I managed a few hours of sleep before we tried again at dawn. Things still were too hot for our crew to unload its gun. It was 10 o'clock in the morning before we finally made the pier at Betio and even though the battle was at its height on the beach, nothing ever felt so good as the solid earth beneath me. This was Sunday – and my forty-first birthday! I felt sure it would be my last.

My recollection of the next three days is very hazy. I managed to keep alive and to keep my cameras working while I inched my way from hole to hole and tree to tree. It really didn't matter which way I aimed the lens – it was bound to cover action in any direction. It was a photographer's paradise – in hell!

Every one of the thousands of weapons on that island, both Marine and Jap, was in constant use until its operator was knocked out. One thing in our favour as photographers was the bright sunlight. There were no dark jungles such as the ones which had hampered us on Guadalcanal.

On Wednesday afternoon, after the fighting had ended, our photographers assembled on the beach. We learned one of the regimental photographers had been killed. He was Staff Sergeant Wesley L. Kroenung Jr of South Pasadena, California. Whitey, as we knew him, had made many fine pictures before he fell. Also, Second Lieutenant Ernest A. Matthews Jr of Dallas, Texas, the Division's assistant public relations officer and a photographer as well, had been killed while filming action on the pier. A mortar shell burst directly beneath him. 'Matty' had been my best friend, ever since we filmed Guadalcanal together. But of our headquarters photo section, miraculously, no one had been killed or seriously injured. We all found it hard to believe that our particular group had escaped heavy casualties.

Each man had his individual, spine-chilling experiences to report. I don't believe there ever was another group of men who had been so close to death so often in such a short time. They had put down their cameras only when they had to use their weapons.

Captain Hayward had shot a tremendous amount of Kodachrome. When the film was collected, we found the men had far exceeded our hopes for truly thorough coverage. Some 900 stills had been made! There were 2,500 feet of 35mm black and white with a lesser amount of Technicolor Monopack and about 5,000 feet of 16mm Kodachrome. Each of the men had performed his task faithfully and well.

Makin Island: 27th Infantry, US Army

As part of the overall GALVANIC operation, while the 2nd Marine Division assaulted Tarawa, the US Army's 27th Division, under the command of Major General Ralph C. Smith, was to assault and capture Makin Island (Butaritari). D-Day was set for 20 November, the same date as the 2nd Division USMC D-Day on Tarawa.

Intelligence estimated the Japanese defences were manned by a garrison of 700 to 800 men, not all of whom were combat troops. Only 280 Rikusentai, under the command of Lieutenant Seizo Ishikawa, were combat-trained; the remainder were Air Force personnel or construction workers, mostly Korean forced labourers.

Ralph Smith, with over 7,000 troops at his disposal, although none had seen combat, had a 10-to-1 advantage over the Japanese. It was estimated that the operation should take no more than four days (although General Holland Smith, 5th Amphibious Corps' overall commander, estimated no more than one day).

The assault plan called for landings on two western beaches. RCT-1 (Regimental Combat Team-1) would land on Red Beach 1; RCT-3 would land alongside on Red Beach 2. Once ashore, these two RCTs would advance east to the west tank barrier, which formed the western limit of the Japanese defences positioned in the centre portion of Butaritari, around On Chong Wharf and King's Wharf. Two hours later, RCT-2 was to land on Yellow Beach from the lagoon side of Butaritari, in the centre of the main Japanese defences, cross the island to the south, then swing east and west towards the east and west tank barriers, taking the Japanese defenders from the rear.

RCT-1 and RCT-3 landed according to plan, with almost no opposition except the occasional sniper. Tank support landed and the push eastward towards the west tank barrier began. Progress was slow as the ground from the beach to the tank barrier had been well churned up by the pre-landing shelling and bombing, some of the light tanks bogging down in water-filled shell holes. Although the D-Day first phase line was reached easily, there the advance stalled for the day.

On Yellow Beach, RCT-2 found the going a lot tougher. Only the first waves boated in Amtracs could get over the barrier reef, the remaining troops in Higgins boats had to wade 200 to 300 yards under fire from the Japanese defenders. Some casualties were sustained but nothing like the numbers suffered by the 2nd Marine Division troops on Tarawa.

With the aid of tanks, Yellow Beach head was secured and the advance across the island started, RCT-2 reaching the south shore by midday. By the end of D-Day RCT-1 and 3 had reached their objective and were dug in for the night. RCT-2 had crossed the island, swung east and advanced towards King's Wharf and west to the west tank barrier. On D-Day plus 1 (D+1) Major General Ralph Smith landed on the island and set his command post. RCT-1 and 3 continued their advance eastwards; RCT-1 taking the full front which allowed RCT-3 to go into reserve. RCT-2 advancing eastwards towards the east tank barrier encountered the stiffest resistance around King's Wharf. For the whole of D+1 the US infantry battled the Japanese defenders, but by nightfall the east tank barrier was still in Japanese hands. RCT-2 dug in for the night, confident that the next day would see an end to organized resistance.

On D+1 an incident occurred that would have lasting consequences for relationships between the US Army and US Marine Corps for years to come.

V Amphibious Corps Commander, General Holland Smith, had released the Corps Reserve to General Julian Smith over at Tarawa, where the situation was very much in danger as all the assault waves were pinned down on the beach. Holland Smith asked for a situation update from Ralph Smith on Makin but, receiving no reply, he commandeered an Amtrac and landed on Red Beach in the afternoon of D+1, going straight to Ralph Smith's HQ, CP and passing troops and tanks standing around awaiting orders (these men were of RCT-3 that had been put into reserve). Ralph Smith informed Holland Smith that there was fierce fighting going on to the north of the island. Not convinced, Holland Smith commandeered a Jeep and driver and headed for the front line. Upon arrival he found the front line 'as quiet as Wall Street on a Sunday'. Holland Smith returned to Ralph Smith's CP and gave him a first-hand example of why Holland was known throughout the Marine Corps as 'Howlin' Mad' Smith. Holland Smith sat down with Ralph Smith and issued orders for D+2, spending the night at Ralph Smith's CP, his mood not improved by a sentry firing his rifle at a shadow, causing the bullet to go through his tent. This was not the last time Holland and Ralph Smith crossed swords. On Saipan in 1944 Holland Smith relieved Ralph Smith of his command for 'lack of aggressiveness' when his men failed to keep pace with the Marine units on his left and right flanks. Repercussions were felt all the way to the Pentagon and Holland Smith's career would suffer.

By 09.20 on D+2, preceded by an artillery barrage, the US troops advanced to the east tank barrier and then pushed east towards the eastern tail of Butaritari, but it was not until the morning of D+3 that troops reached the village of Tanimaiki on the eastern tip of the island. At 1130 hours, General Ralph Smith radioed Admiral Turner 'Makin taken'. It had taken seventy-five hours to conquer Makin and its 700 to 800 defenders; almost the same time as it had taken the 2nd Marine Division to take Betio (Tarawa) with more than 4,000 defenders. Casualties were light for the US Army on Makin; not so for the US Navy. During the pre-landing bombardment a turret explosion aboard the USS *Mississippi* killed forty-three sailors. In addition, the escort carrier USS *Liscome Bay* was sunk by the Japanese submarine *I-175*. A single torpedo struck the *Liscome Bay*, detonating its aircraft bomb stockpile. The explosion engulfed the whole of the *Liscome Bay*, which sank in minutes. Of the 916 crew members on board, only 272 were rescued.

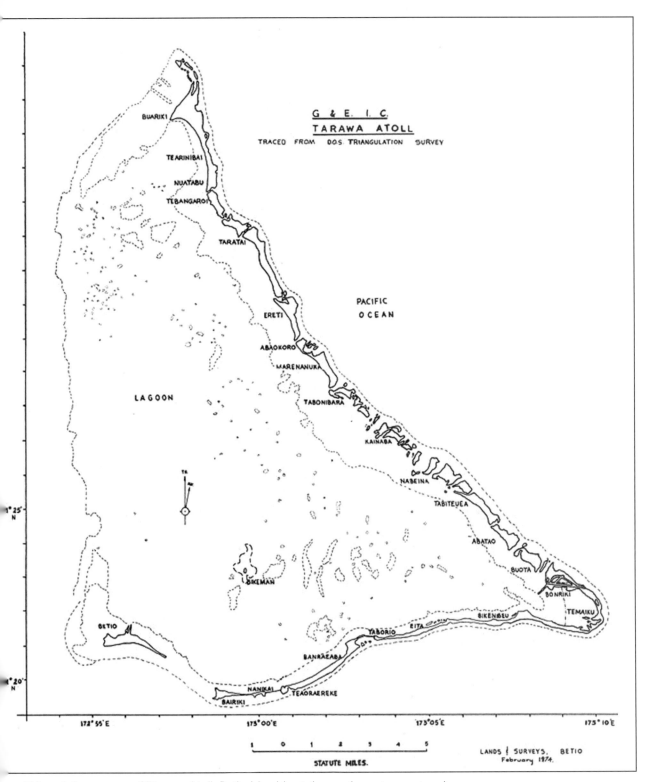

Triangulation survey of Tarawa Atoll, Betio Island is at the south-western extremity.

Aerial view of Betio Island taken by USAAF reconnaissance aircraft prior to the assault in November 1943.

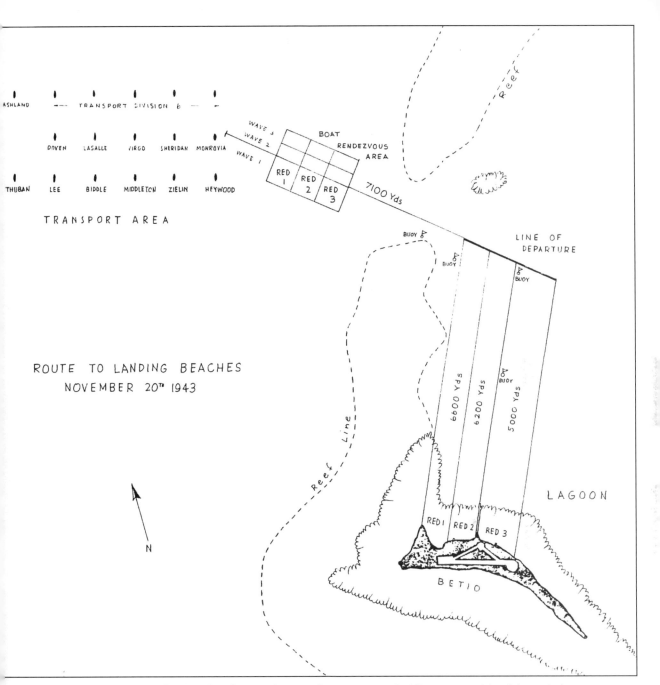

The proposed route to landing beaches for assault waves from transport holding area outside of the main lagoon to 'line of departure'. Only the first three assault waves would be boated in Amtracs, LVT-1s and LVT-2s. Following assault waves including artillery and tanks would be boated in landing craft LCVPs and LCMs incapable of crossing the barrier reef some 600 to 700 yards from the beaches.

Religious services held for the assault troops on the day before D-Day on Betio.

Pilots of VF-16 being briefed aboard the USS *Lexington* off Tarawa Atoll, 20 November 1943.

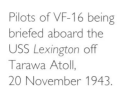

Aircraft warm up aboard the USS *Yorktown*, 20 November 1943 (D-Day), off Tarawa Atoll.

Landing craft circle at the line of departure prior to the run-in to the assault beaches on Betio on D-Day. Due to the low tide over the barrier reef, none of the LCVPs or LCMs could cross. Tanks in the LCMs had been waterproofed and were able to launch at the reef line, but infantry on the LCVPs had to wait for returning Amtracs to carry them to the beaches or wade the 700 yards from the reef to the beaches. Betio can be seen in the far distance.

D-Day on Betio Island. Landing craft circle at the line of departure awaiting a signal to head in to the beaches. The landing craft LCVPs and LCMs would not be able to cross the inner reef some 700 yards from the beach and troops would have to wait for returning LVTs to ship them onto the beaches or wade the 700 yards under heavy fire from numerous Japanese weapons.

'Whisky Sour', LVT-1 No. 28, heads into the landing beaches on D-Day, 20 November. The first three waves of assault troops were boated in Amtracs, LVT-1s or LVT-2s.

Rear Admiral Keiji Shibasaki arrived on Betio in September 1943. Young and ambitious, a veteran in amphibious landings in China, he wasted no time in upgrading all-round defences on Betio. Taken by surprise when the US landed on the northern beaches, he had expected the invasion would come from the south. He swiftly moved men from the south to man defensive positions on the northern beaches. Shibasaki's death in the afternoon of D-Day was a major blow to the Japanese defenders. His claim of the 'The Americans could not take Tarawa with a million men in a hundred years' would be proved wrong; it took the 2nd Marine Division seventy-six hours!

(**Opposite, above**) D-Day on Red Beach 2. Marines take cover at the sea wall. LVT-1 No. 45 has been put out of action at the sea wall. Almost half of the Amtracs were immobilized by Japanese fire on D-Day.

(**Opposite, below**) D-Day on Red Beach 1. Marines take cover wherever they can, there being no sea wall on Red 1 to provide cover. In the background can be seen the long pier and disabled Amtracs. Overhead, navy and Marine aircraft bomb and strafe Japanese positions.

(**Above**) It was late in the afternoon of D-Day that the 10th Marines (artillery) attempted to land their guns. Unable to cross the barrier reef in Higgins boats and few Amtracs being available, they landed their guns on the long pier and attempted to move them down the pier to Red Beach 2, suffering casualties as the pier was still under heavy small-arms fire from the Japanese defenders.

The 10th Marines suffered many casualties trying to move their guns down the long pier to Red Beach 2. Several dead Marines can be seen with others using one of the 75mm Pack Howitzers for cover. The eastern tail end of Betio can be seen in the background.

Support waves in LCVPs circle at the line of departure, awaiting orders to move into the beaches, unaware of what awaits them at the barrier reef. One Marine even finds time to show off his pin-up girlfriend (who has probably never heard of him!).

Marines take shelter from the murderous Japanese small-arms fire at the sea wall on Red Beach 2. Disabled Amtracs are in the distance, also one of the few M4-A2 Sherman tanks that had made it to the beach. The Shermans had been waterproofed and were able to get from the barrier reef to the beaches, although some fell foul of shell holes in the lagoon and drowned out. In the far distance is the long pier, which afforded some cover to Marines attempting to reach the beaches from the barrier reef.

Assistant machine-gunners on Red Beach 3 strip .30 calibre machine-gun belts from dead comrades during D-Day. Due to the murderous Japanese fire all along the beachhead, supplies of ammunition, water and medical supplies were at a premium.

(**Above, left**) Colonel David M. Shoup, USMC at his CP on Red Beach 2, Betio, his trademark cigar clenched in his teeth. As operations officer, Shoup formulated the assault on Tarawa. During the planning stage, Shoup had concerns about the surrounding reef on Betio; his solution was to use LVT amphibious tractors for at least the first three assault waves. With the assistance of Major Henry Drewes commanding the 2nd Amphibious Tractor Battalion, Shoup managed to scrounge seventy-five old LVT-1s with a further fifty LVT-2s being shipped direct from the manufacturer Stateside. Rehearsals were held at Efate and it was here that Colonel William Marshall, commanding Combat Team 2, suffered a heart attack and was shipped home to the United States. General Holland Smith promoted Shoup from lieutenant colonel to colonel and had him take command of CT2. Shoup would perform brilliantly on Tarawa, despite his being wounded on the way in to the beaches on D-Day. He would later be awarded the Medal of Honor for his conduct on Betio; one of four such medals awarded to the 2nd Marine Division and the only one not awarded posthumously.

(**Above, right**) First Lieutenant William Deane Hawkins, USMC joined the Marine Corps in 1941 and, following a series of rapid promotions, attained the rank of first lieutenant by the time of the assault on Tarawa. Put in command of a thirty-six-strong scout/sniper platoon whose first assignment on D-Day at Tarawa was to land ahead of the first assault waves at the long pier situated between Red Beaches 1 and 2, the pier was successfully cleared of Japanese defenders. Hawkins landed his team on Red 2 and immediately set about assaulting Japanese strongpoints around the airstrip. During these attacks Hawkins was wounded in the hand by a Japanese mortar round, the round killing three of his men. Hawkins refused medical attention and continued with his attacks on the airstrip strongpoints. It was here that Hawkins received further wounds in the shoulder and chest from a Japanese machine gun; he was taken back to a field hospital on Red 2 but died from his wounds during the night of D-Day. His Medal of Honor citation reads: 'WILLIAM DEANE HAWKINS, First Lieutenant, USMC, 2d Marines, November 20–21, 1943, Died of Wounds. For valorous and gallant conduct above and beyond the call of duty as Commanding Officer of a Scout Sniper Platoon attached to the Assault Regiment in action against Japanese-held Tarawa in the Gilbert Islands, 20 and 21 November 1943. The first to disembark from the jeep lighter, First Lieutenant Hawkins unhesitatingly moved forward under heavy enemy fire at the end of the Betio Pier, neutralizing emplacements in coverage of troops assaulting the main beach positions. Fearlessly leading his men on to join the forces fighting desperately to gain a beachhead, he repeatedly risked his life throughout the day and night to direct and lead attacks on pillboxes and installations with grenades and demolitions. At dawn on the following day, First Lieutenant Hawkins resumed the dangerous mission of clearing the limited beachhead of Japanese resistance, personally initiating an assault on a hostile position fortified by five machine guns, fired point-blank into the loopholes and completed the destruction with grenades. Refusing to withdraw after being seriously wounded in the chest during this skirmish, First Lieutenant Hawkins steadfastly carried the fight to the enemy, destroying three more pillboxes before he was caught in a burst of Japanese shellfire and mortally wounded. His relentless fighting spirit in the face of formidable opposition and his exceptionally daring tactics served as an inspiration to his comrades during the most crucial phase of the battle and reflect the highest credit upon the United States Naval Service. He gallantly gave his life for his country.'

An LVT-2 is hoisted back aboard its transport ship for repairs during D-Day, this being one of the few damaged Amtracs to make it back to the transports after landing troops on the beaches.

(**Opposite, above**) LCVPs unable to cross the barrier reef land supplies and ammunition at the end of the long pier, which then had to be manhandled down the pier under Japanese sniper fire to the beaches.

(**Opposite, below**) Colonel Shoup's command post on Red Beach 2, set up early on the morning of D-Day at the back of a Japanese bunker. Shoup was to command the battle from this bunker until relieved by Colonel Edson on D+1. Shoup stayed on the island, despite his infected wounds sustained on D-Day, as Edson's assistant throughout the remainder of the battle.

(**Above**) The sea wall on Red Beaches 2 and 3 (there was no sea wall on Red Beach 1) provided the best protection to the assaulting Marines on D-Day. Here groups and individual Marines go over the top to assault Japanese emplacements with rifles, demolition charges and flame-throwers, while other Marines recover from the ordeal of landing.

David Shoup's command post on Red Beach 2. Shoup (centre, holding map) consults with his fellow officers. Sitting on the ground beside Shoup is Colonel Evans Carlson (of Carlson's Raiders' fame), there as an observer from the 4th Marine Division (Carlson no longer commanded the 2nd Raider Battalion). During D-Day Carlson waded several times through the lagoon to the barrier reef with messages from Shoup to Julian Smith, who was still afloat when radio communication failed. In the background (hand on hip) is another Raider legend, Colonel Merritt 'Red Mike' Edson, Divisional Chief of Staff. Edson joined Shoup and took over command at 2030 hours on D+1.

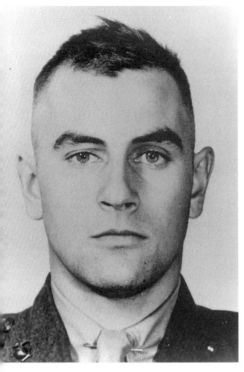

Staff Sergeant William J. Bordelon, USMC was posthumously awarded the Medal of Honor for his actions on D-Day, 20 November 1943, on Tarawa (Betio). His citation stated: 'WILLIAM JAMES BORDELON, Staff Sergeant USMC, A Company, 18th Marines, November 20, 1943, Killed In Action. For valorous and gallant conduct above and beyond the call of duty as a Member of an Assault Engineer Platoon of the First Battalion, Eighteenth Marines, tactically attached to the Second Marine Division in action against the Japanese-held atoll of Tarawa in the Gilbert Islands on 20 November 1943. Landing in the assault waves under withering enemy fire which killed all but four of the men in his tractor, Staff Sergeant Bordelon hurriedly made demolition charges and personally put two pillboxes out of action. Hit by enemy machine-gun fire just as a charge exploded in his hand while assaulting a third position, he unhesitatingly went to the aid of one of his demolition men, wounded and calling for help in the water, rescuing this man and another who had been hit by enemy fire while attempting to make the rescue. Still refusing first-aid for himself, he again made up demolition charges and single-handedly assaulted a fourth Japanese machine-gun position but was instantly killed when caught in a final burst of fire from the enemy. Staff Sergeant Bordelon's great personal valor during a critical phase of securing the limited beachhead was a contributing factor in the ultimate occupation of the island and his heroic determination throughout three days of violent battle reflects the highest credit upon the United States Naval Service. He gallantly gave his life for his country.

Colonel David Monroe Shoup, USMC. The only one of four Medal of Honor recipients to be alive at the end of the battle for Tarawa, Shoup's Medal of Honor citation stated: 'DAVID MONROE SHOUP, Colonel, USMC, Command-ing Officer, 2d Marines, November 20–22, 1943. For conspicuous gallantry and intrepidity at the risk of his life above and beyond the call of duty as Commanding Officer of all Marine Corps troops in action against enemy

Japanese forces on Betio Island, Tarawa Atoll, Gilbert Islands from 20 to 22 November 1943. Although severely shocked by an exploding enemy shell soon after landing at the pier, and suffering from a serious, painful leg wound which had become infected, Colonel Shoup fearlessly exposed himself to the terrific and relentless artillery, machine-gun and rifle fire from hostile shore emplacements. Rallying his hesitant troops by his own inspiring heroism, he gallantly led them across the fringing reefs to charge the heavily fortified island and reinforce our hard-pressed, thinly-held lines. Upon arrival on shore, he assumed command of all landed troops and, working without rest under constant, withering enemy fire during the next two days, conducted smashing attacks against unbelievably strong and fanatically defended Japanese positions despite innumerable obstacles and heavy casualties. By his brilliant leadership, daring tactics and selfless devotion to duty, Colonel Shoup was largely responsible for the final decisive defeat of the enemy and his indomitable fighting spirit reflects great credit upon the United States Naval Service.'

(**Above**) V Amphibious Corps Commander Holland M. 'Howlin' Mad' Smith (left) and Divisional Commander Julian Smith (right) tour the newly-captured Betio Island.

(**Opposite, below**) On the evening of D-Day, the 10th Marines (artillery), boated in LCVPs, managed to land some of their 75mm Pack Howitzers and 37mm anti-tank guns onto the end of the long pier. It was intended to set up the 75mm howitzers on Red Beach 2, able to cover most of Betio. During the night of D-Day/D+1, the 10th Marine gunners manhandled the 37mm anti-tank guns down the pier and disassembled the 75mm Pack Howitzers and carried them through the lagoon to Red Beach 2. By the morning of D+1 the guns were in place and ready to give support where needed.

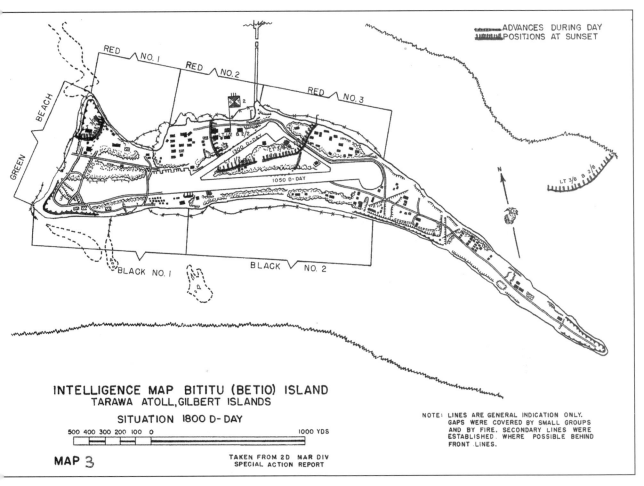

INTELLIGENCE MAP BITITU (BETIO) ISLAND
TARAWA ATOLL, GILBERT ISLANDS

SITUATION 1800 D-DAY

RED NO. 1
RED NO. 2
RED NO. 3
GREEN BEACH
BLACK NO. 1
BLACK NO. 2

ADVANCES DURING DAY
POSITIONS AT SUNSET

1800 D-DAY
1050 D-DAY

LT 3/8 8 2/8

500 400 300 200 100 0   1000 YDS

MAP 3

TAKEN FROM 2D MAR DIV
SPECIAL ACTION REPORT

NOTE: LINES ARE GENERAL INDICATION ONLY.
GAPS WERE COVERED BY SMALL GROUPS
AND BY FIRE. SECONDARY LINES WERE
ESTABLISHED WHERE POSSIBLE BEHIND
FRONT LINES.

(**Above**) Recovered from the shock of the landings on D-Day, Marines all along the beachhead began to move inland, taking the fight to the Japanese defenders. Here a platoon leader, wounded in the hand, cradles his rifle, leading his men past barbed-wire entanglements.

(**Opposite, above**) On all the beaches, groups of Marines sought out Japanese defences and attacked with rifles, machine guns, explosives and flame-throwers. Here a squad leader has identified yet another Japanese strongpoint for his men to assault.

(**Opposite, below**) On Red Beach 3, Marines with fixed bayonets move inland past a disabled Amtrac.

(**Above**) Makeshift aid stations were set up on the beaches. Here a wounded Marine received blood plasma from a navy corpsman prior to being transferred back to waiting transports for further medical attention.

(**Opposite, above**) Having cleared out Japanese defenders, these Marines have set up a .30 calibre machine gun. Two Marines take a rest and a drink of water while another Marine throws a hand grenade at their next objective.

(**Opposite, below**) On Red Beach 3 Major Henry 'Jim' Crowe (centre) consults with his company commanders ready to push east and west from their positions on the beach. Jim Crowe, a fiery commander, led his men valiantly on Tarawa, though it was said by some that his men feared him more than the Japanese!

(**Above**) The biggest advances by Marines on D+1 was by a motley collection of infantry, Amtrac drivers, heavy weapons engineers and corpsmen rounded up on Red Beach 1 on D-Day by Major Michael Ryan, 2nd Marines. On D+1 Ryan and the composite battalion pushed along Green Beach on the west end of Betio, taking Japanese defences from the flanks and rear (most defensive positions' guns pointed out to sea). By the end of D+1, Ryan and his men had reached the 8in Vickers gun emplacements on Temakin Point at the far south-west of Betio. The Marines now had a landing beach completely in their hands. Colonel Shoup was able to send Julian Smith a situation report informing him that Green Beach was in Marine hands to some 150 yards inland. All elements on Red Beaches 1, 2 and 3 were advancing inland and he finished his report with his assessment: 'Casualties many, percentage dead not known, combat efficiency – WE ARE WINNING!'. In contrast, at the end of D+1 a last radio message was received from the Betio defenders: 'Our weapons have been destroyed. From now on everyone is attempting a final charge. May Japan exist for a thousand years.'

(**Opposite, below**) D+2. Reinforcements arrive on Green Beach. Major Ryan had established a defensive line the whole width of Green Beach some 200 yards inland.

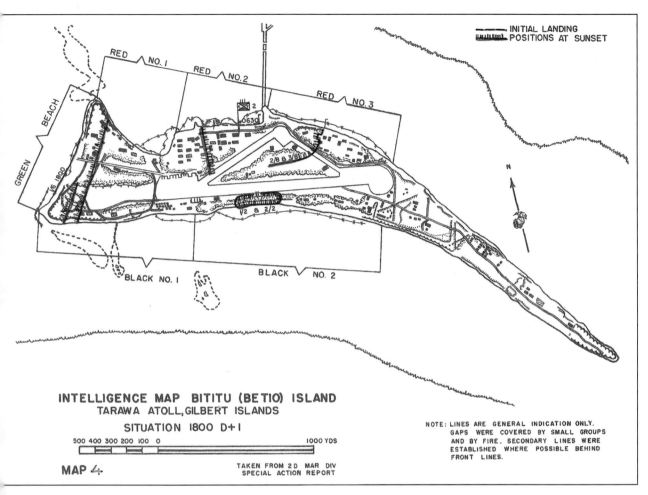

RED NO. 1

RED NO. 2

RED NO. 3

GREEN BEACH

2
063

2/8 & 3/6

V2 & 2/2

N

BLACK NO. I

BLACK NO. 2

INTELLIGENCE MAP BITITU (BETIO) ISLAND
TARAWA ATOLL, GILBERT ISLANDS

SITUATION 1800 D+1

500 400 300 200 100 0   1000 YDS

MAP 4

TAKEN FROM 2D MAR DIV
SPECIAL ACTION REPORT

NOTE: LINES ARE GENERAL INDICATION ONLY.
GAPS WERE COVERED BY SMALL GROUPS
AND BY FIRE. SECONDARY LINES WERE
ESTABLISHED WHERE POSSIBLE BEHIND
FRONT LINES.

(**Above**) All along the Red Beaches, Marines push inland taking out Japanese defensive positions. Utter devastation as seen here was typical all over Betio.

(**Opposite, above**) On Red Beach 3, Major Crowe's composite 2/8, 3/8 Regiment attacked inland and to the west to join with Red 2 and to the east along the tail of the island. To the west, Crowe was held up by a huge defensive sand-covered bunker. Attached to Crowe's 2/8, 3/8 were elements of the 18th Marines (Engineers), led by First Lieutenant Alexander Bonnyman. Bonnyman devised a plan to assault the bunker with his engineers, supported by Crowe's infantry. Bonnyman had observed that the top of the bunker had several air vents; his intention was to drop explosive charges and fire flame-throwers down these vents. Here Marines are checking for any Japanese survivors of the assault. In the centre background is a combat cameraman. Film footage of the assault would win prizes for the Marines in 1944 after the battle.

(**Opposite, below**) Reinforcements wade ashore alongside one of several Japanese latrines on Green Beach. Concrete tetrahedrons can be seen in the far background.

By D+2 Marines on all fronts were advancing inland, the issue no longer in doubt.

First Lieutenant Alexander Bonnyman Jr, USMC commanded 'C' Company, 18th Marines on Betio. Attached to Jim Crowe's 8th Marines, Bonnyman led the successful assault on the huge Japanese bunker on the west end of Red Beach 3 on D+2. Posthumously awarded the Medal of Honor for his actions, his citation is as follows: 'ALEXANDER BONNYMAN JR, First Lieutenant, USMCR, C Company, 18th Marines, November 20–22, 1943, Killed in Action. For conspicuous gallantry and intrepidity at the risk of his life above and beyond the call of duty as Executive Officer of the Second Battalion Shore Party, Eighth Marines, Second Marine Division, during the assault against enemy Japanese-held Tarawa in the Gilbert Islands, 20–22 November 1943. Acting on his own initiative when assault troops were pinned down at the far end of Betio Pier by the overwhelming fire of Japanese shore batteries, First Lieutenant Bonnyman

repeatedly defied the blasting fury of the enemy bombardment to organize and lead the besieged men over the long, open pier to the beach and then, voluntarily obtaining flame-throwers and demolitions, organized his pioneer shore party into assault demolitionists and directed the blowing of several hostile installations before the close of D-Day. Determined to effect an opening in the enemy's strongly-organized defense line the following day, he voluntarily crawled approximately forty yards forward of our lines and placed demolitions in the entrance of a large Japanese emplacement as the initial move in his planned attack against the heavily garrisoned, bombproof installation which was stubbornly resisting despite the destruction early in the action of a large number of Japanese who had been inflicting casualties on our forces and holding up our advance. Withdrawing only to replenish his ammunition, he led his men in a renewed assault, fearlessly exposing himself to the merciless slash of hostile fire as he stormed the formidable bastion, directed the placement of demolition charges in both entrances, and seized the top of the bombproof position, flushing more than 100 of the enemy who were instantly cut down, and effecting the annihilation of approximately 150 troops inside the emplacement. Assailed by additional Japanese after he had gained his objective, he made a heroic stand on the edge of the structure, defending his strategic position with indomitable determination in the face of desperate charge and killing three of the enemy before he fell, mortally wounded. By his dauntless spirit, unrelenting aggressiveness and forceful leadership throughout three days of unremitting, violent battle, First Lieutenant Bonnyman had inspired his men to heroic effort, enabling them to beat off the counterattack and break the back of hostile resistance in that sector for an immediate gain of 400 yards with no further casualties to our forces in this zone. He gallantly gave his life for his country.

Red Beach 3, the assault on the huge bunker at the west end of Red 3, led by First Lieutenant Bonnyman and his 'forlorn hope' engineers. Bonnyman is on the centre crest with carbine and no helmet cover.

Red Beach 3. Marines mop up after Lieutenant Bonnyman has successfully taken out the huge sand-covered bunker. Some 150 dead Japanese were counted around the bunker with a further 200 dead inside.

Green Beach, Betio. Aerial view taken after the island had been secured. Note rubber boats at centre on the beach used to ferry reinforcements to shore also to remove wounded off the island.

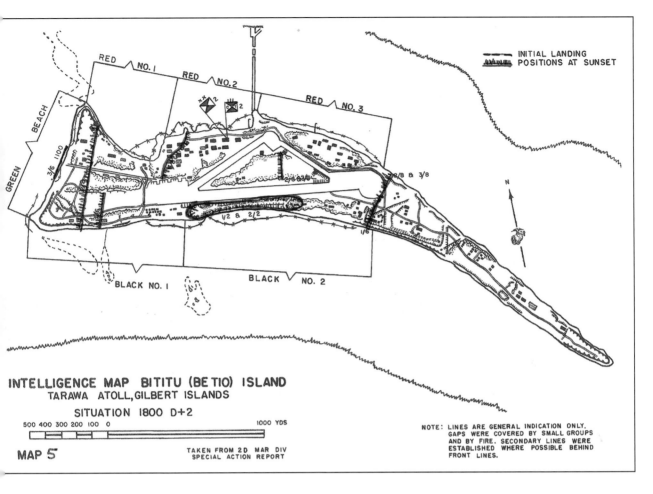

INTELLIGENCE MAP BITITU (BETIO) ISLAND
TARAWA ATOLL, GILBERT ISLANDS
SITUATION 1800 D+2

500 400 300 200 100 0   1000 YDS

MAP 5   TAKEN FROM 2D MAR DIV
                        SPECIAL ACTION REPORT

RED   NO. 1
RED   NO. 2
RED   NO. 3
GREEN BEACH
BLACK NO. 1
BLACK   NO. 2

INITIAL LANDING
POSITIONS AT SUNSET

N

NOTE: LINES ARE GENERAL INDICATION ONLY.
GAPS WERE COVERED BY SMALL GROUPS
AND BY FIRE. SECONDARY LINES WERE
ESTABLISHED WHERE POSSIBLE BEHIND
FRONT LINES.

D+3 saw the assault on the final Japanese pocket of resistance. The pocket, a group of inter-supporting emplacements at the junction between Red Beach 1 and Red Beach 2, had so far resisted all attempts to destroy it. Here, infantry on Red Beach 2 prepare for the final assault on the pocket.

With the pocket secured, all organized Japanese resistance had gone. Here around the outer grounds surrounding the pocket are some of the hundreds of dead Rikusentai.

D+3. Following the failed Japanese 'Banzai' charge against Jones's 1/6 on the night of D+2/D+3, men of McLeod's 3/6 advanced rapidly towards the eastern tail of Betio.

By D+3 wounded could safely be transferred from rubber boats to LCVPs at the barrier reef and onto troop transports for further medical attention.

D+3. The island by now was covered with dead, both Marine and Japanese, rotting in the blistering heat. Here Marines check out a dead Rikusentai, mindful that the corpse could be 'booby-trapped'.

The easiest way to transport the wounded to waiting LCVPs at the barrier reef was by rubber boat, the tides still not allowing LCVPs into the lagoon and up to the beaches.

Noon, 24 November (D+3). Men prepare to hoist the Stars and Stripes over Betio. Later that day, a British Union Jack was located and run up next to 'Old Glory', signifying the return of British rule to the Gilbert Islands.

With the island declared secure, Marines in rear areas on the now quiet beaches take time to reflect on the past seventy-six hours.

It was said that the issue was no longer in doubt when the first Jeep landed on the beaches.

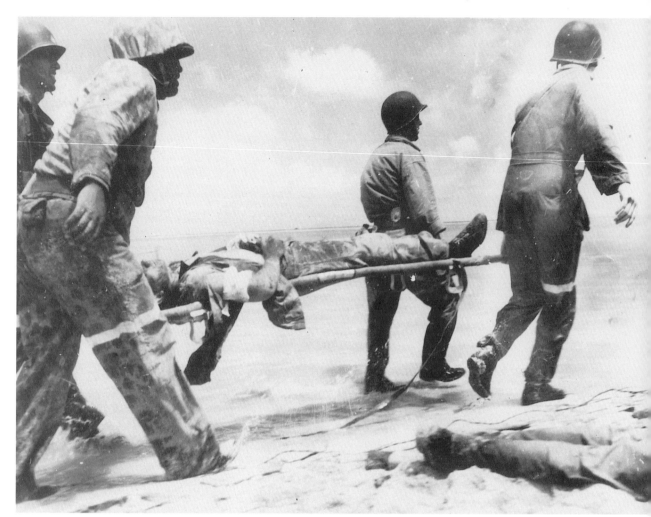

At last the wounded could be moved from the makeshift aid stations on the beaches to the waiting transports. Here a stretcher party passes a dead Marine, oblivious to his presence (the dead would have to wait).

Medical Corpsmen, naval personnel attached to the Marines (the Marines did not have medical personnel of their own, unlike the army). The white discs on clothing and helmets identify them as corpsmen. The corpsmen had taken to using white discs as opposed to red crosses on armbands and helmets due to – on Guadalcanal – the red crosses making a good target for Japanese snipers.

The Stars and Stripes flies over Betio. The palm tree on the left would later fly the British Union Jack.

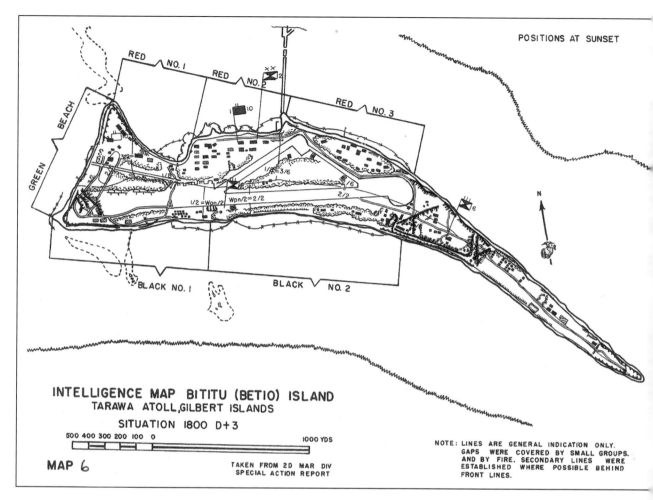

RED NO. 1
RED NO. 2
RED NO. 3
GREEN BEACH
BLACK NO. 1
BLACK NO. 2

1/2 = Wpn/2
Wpn/2 = 2/2
1/8 3/6
3/6
2/2

N

INTELLIGENCE MAP BITITU (BETIO) ISLAND
TARAWA ATOLL, GILBERT ISLANDS
SITUATION 1800 D+3

500 400 300 200 100 0   1000 YDS

MAP 6

TAKEN FROM 2D MAR DIV
SPECIAL ACTION REPORT

NOTE: LINES ARE GENERAL INDICATION ONLY.
GAPS WERE COVERED BY SMALL GROUPS,
AND BY FIRE. SECONDARY LINES WERE
ESTABLISHED WHERE POSSIBLE BEHIND
FRONT LINES.

(**Right**) The first pilot to land on Betio is welcomed by Marines on the airstrip, even though Seabees were still working on it.

(**Opposite, above**) Once the island had been declared secured, the clean-up could begin in earnest. The whole of the island of Betio was a lunar landscape of shell holes and debris, not to mention more than 4,000 corpses to be buried. Here a Marine corpse is carried for burial in one of the many cemeteries. A wooden door panel is used as a makeshift stretcher.

(**Opposite, below**) In many of the Japanese bunkers the defenders had chosen death by their own hand rather than capture. Here two Rikusentai have committed suicide by placing their rifle to the forehead and pulling the trigger with their toe.

(**Above**) Every Japanese emplacement had to be checked for booby traps and live Rikusentai for days after the island was declared secure.

(**Opposite, above**) Green Beach has become a rest area for Marines awaiting transport away from Betio. The assault troops were quickly replaced by garrison troops and shipped to Hawaii for R & R.

(**Opposite, below**) Admiral Shibasaki's command bunker on the north side of Betio. A three-storey reinforced concrete structure, it was outside this bunker that Shibasaki and his officers were killed on D-Day while transferring to the south side of the island. The bunker withstood even 16in shells from battleships, only being eliminated by explosive charges or gasoline.

(**Opposite, above**) Walking wounded were able to walk down the long pier (in the background) to get a transfer by Higgins boat to waiting transport ships.

(**Opposite, below**) A tin shed panel is used as a stretcher for a decomposing Marine corpse. It was said that the stench could be smelled 30 miles away from Betio.

(**Above**) Wounded, this is one of the few Rikusentai to surrender, stripped down to his loin cloth just in case he was harbouring a weapon or grenade. Only seven Japanese troops were taken alive, the remaining PoWs being Korean forced labour who took little part in the fighting.

Debris of war: LVT-1s and a Japanese Type 95 Ha-Go tank now litter the beaches.

Wreckage of Japanese aircraft, probably destroyed by the pre-invasion bombing by the USAAF 7th Air Force from the Ellice Islands, litter Betio's airstrip.

Navy medical personnel would operate on Marine and Japanese wounded alike. Here two corpsmen work on a wounded Rikusentai, one of the few taken alive.

(**Opposite, above**) Korean forced labourers: most hid from the carnage on Betio, although a few did assist the Japanese defenders as carriers but they carried no weapons.

(**Above**) Friend and foe alike lay dead side by side while exhausted Marines rest in the background, oblivious to the carnage surrounding them. PTSD did not exist in 1943!

(**Opposite, below**) Curious Marines inspect Japanese guns. Now silent, these guns wreaked havoc on D-Day.

(**Above**) Everywhere on Betio there were rotting corpses in urgent need of burial. Here Japanese troops had been caught in the open by Marine riflemen and flame-throwers.

(**Opposite, above**) Huge crater caused by a direct hit on this Japanese 5in shell store on Betio.

(**Opposite, below**) Not many of the buildings around the airfield on Betio survived the battle.

Curious Marines investigate a Japanese Type 95 Ha-Go tank in a revetment on the airfield.

Marines take time to rest after the island has been declared taken. Burial parties begin to identify and bury fallen comrades.

Captured Korean forced labourers being taken to the PoW holding pen by the long pier on Betio.

Marine and navy officers find time to tour Betio Island.

(**Above**) Left to right: Brigadier General Thomas Bourke, 10th Marines; Colonel Merritt Edson, Chief of Staff and Major General Julian Smith, Commander General 2nd Marine Division after the battle for Betio.

(**Opposite, above**) Aerial view of Betio after the battle. Hardly a single palm tree is left standing. In the centre are coconut log revetments for aircraft at the side of the airstrip. In the background can be seen numerous disabled Amtracs of Red Beach 1.

(**Opposite, below**) LVT-1 and LVT-2 wrecked at the sea wall on Red Beach 2. Note high tide and Marine corpse floating. LVT-1 'My Dolores' #49 was the first LVT onto the beaches on D-Day. After the battle she was recovered and shipped Stateside to take part in War Bond tours. 'My Dolores' ended her days at Camp Pendleton after the war.

(**Opposite, above**) Aerial view of the eastern tail of Betio after the battle. Note the high tank barrier on the right stretching right across the island. It made a useful burial trench for Japanese dead.

(**Above**) Disabled Amtracs at the sea wall and in the lagoon on Red Beaches 1 and 2. Marine dead still float in the lagoon awaiting recovery.

(**Opposite, below**) 'Goodbye Tarawa.' Assault troops march down to the pier to await transports that will ship them to their new home on Big Island, Hawaii.

(**Above**) Japanese dead litter this bunker, reduced by explosive charges and flame-throwers.

(**Opposite, above**) Within days, the Seabees had Betio airstrip (now called Hawkins Field after Lieutenant Dean Hawkins MOH (posthumous)) ready to receive aircraft. Here a Hellcat lands, passing the remains of a Japanese plane that will never fly again.

(**Opposite, below**) Korean labourers carry their own dead and wounded to receive medical treatment or burial in mass graves along with Japanese dead.

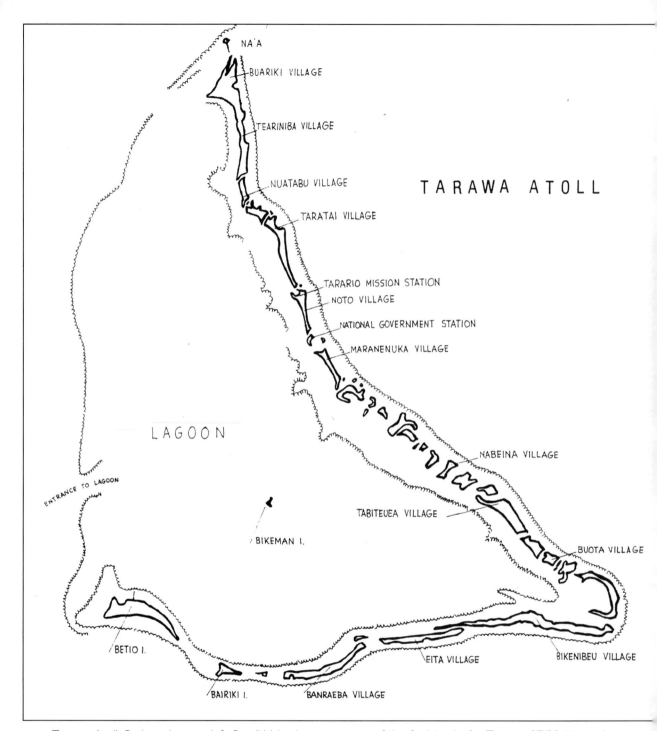

NA'A

BUARIKI VILLAGE

TEARINIBA VILLAGE

NUATABU VILLAGE

TARATAI VILLAGE

TARARIO MISSION STATION

NOTO VILLAGE

NATIONAL GOVERNMENT STATION

MARANENUKA VILLAGE

TARAWA ATOLL

LAGOON

ENTRANCE TO LAGOON

NABEINA VILLAGE

TABITEUEA VILLAGE

BIKEMAN I.

BUOTA VILLAGE

BETIO I.

BIKENIBEU VILLAGE

EITA VILLAGE

BAIRIKI I.

BANRAEBA VILLAGE

Tarawa Atoll, Betio at bottom left; Buariki Island at top: scene of the final battle for Tarawa, 27/28 November.

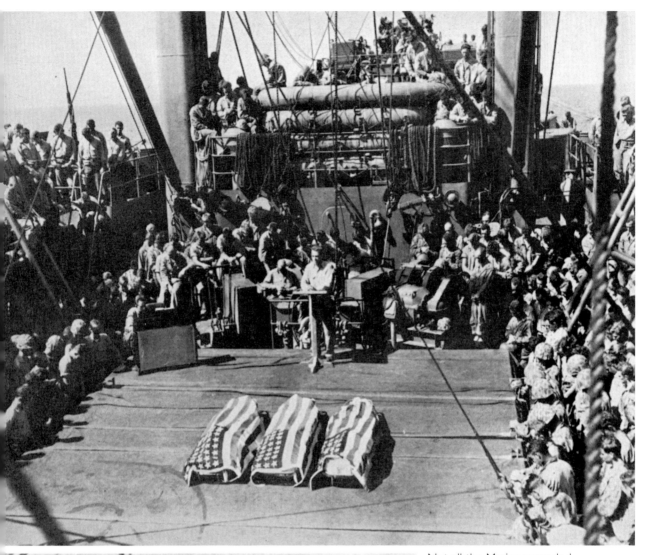

Not all the Marine wounded survived. Here three Marines are given burials at sea with full military honours on board one of the transports.

Captain Louis Hayward, former Hollywood movie star, joined the Marine Corps in July 1942. Most of the amazing movie footage on Tarawa was taken by Hayward himself.

Sergeant Ferman Dixon, combat photographer, examines a damaged Shinto shrine after the battle on Betio.

Corporal Obie Newcomb, combat photographer, landed with the first waves of assault troops on Betio.

Combat photographer Obie Newcomb and Raymond Matjasic take time out by the wreckage of a Japanese plane on Betio's airstrip.

Combat photographers not only carried a camera into combat. Here cameraman Obie Newcomb, armed with rifle, bayonet and hand grenades, takes time out for a well-earned drink of water.

Amazingly, numerous animals survived the battle for Tarawa. Here a pig is patched up by a navy corpsman, photographed by a combat cameraman after the island was secured.

A Marine looks longingly at a native chicken that has survived the battle, but may not survive the aftermath.

Captain Hayward's photographic unit after the battle. Strained faces and forced smiles hide the slaughter these men have witnessed and recorded on film.

Garrison troops found a use for Japanese dugouts, here re-named 'The lousy, lousy lounge' near the airstrip on Betio.

'Siwash the Duck', the beer-drinking mascot of the 1st Battalion, 10th Marines, and later of the whole of the 2nd Marine Division, landed on Tarawa. Upon landing on the beach, he engaged in combat with a Japanese-owned rooster, sustaining injuries but victorious. Later cited by his fellow Marines, his citation read: 'For courageous action and wounds received on Tarawa, in the Gilbert Islands, November 1943. With utter disregard for his own personal safety, Siwash, upon reaching the beach, without hesitation engaged the enemy in fierce combat, namely one rooster of Japanese ancestry, and though wounded on the head by repeated pecks, he soon routed the opposition. He refused medical aid until all wounded members of his section had been taken care of.' After the war, Siwash retired to a farm but returned to the Corps as a recruiter for the Marine Corps during the Korean War.

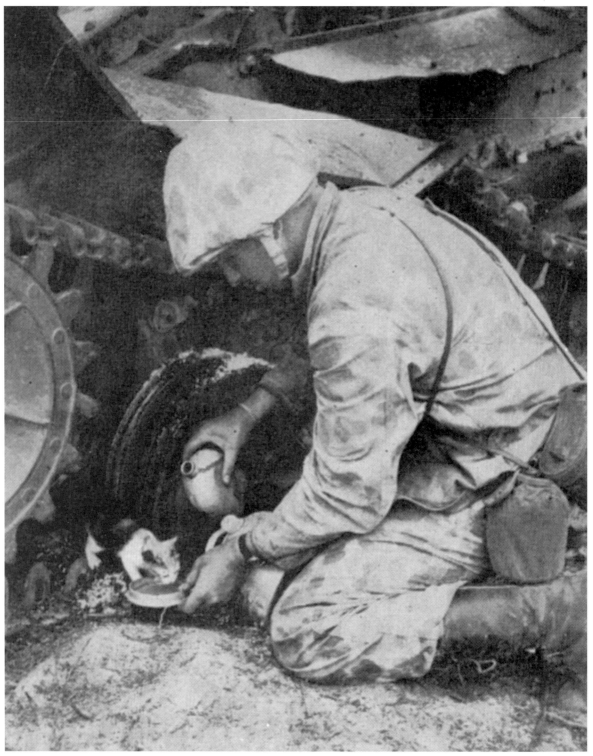

After all the carnage of the past seventy-six hours, this Marine finds time to share his precious water with a terrified kitten hiding under a knocked-out Japanese tank.

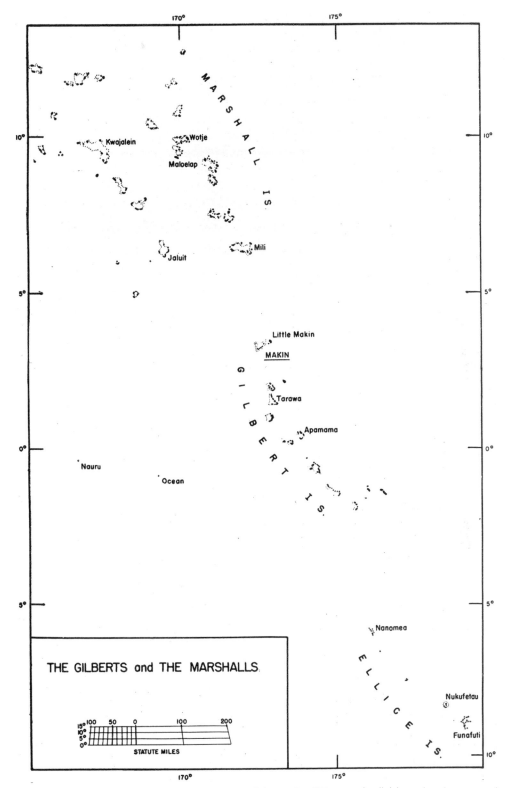

Gilbert and Ellice Islands: Makin Atoll (Butaritari) is north of Tarawa Atoll. Note the closeness of the Japanese-held Marshall Islands to the Gilbert Islands.

MAIN DEFENSIVE AREA
OF BUTARITARI

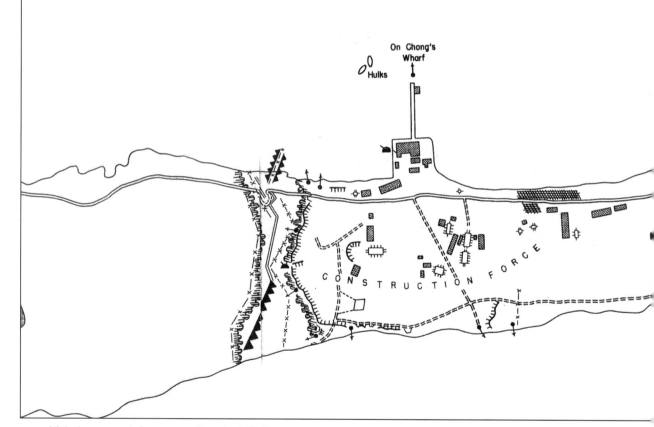

Main Japanese defence area, Butaritari 1943.

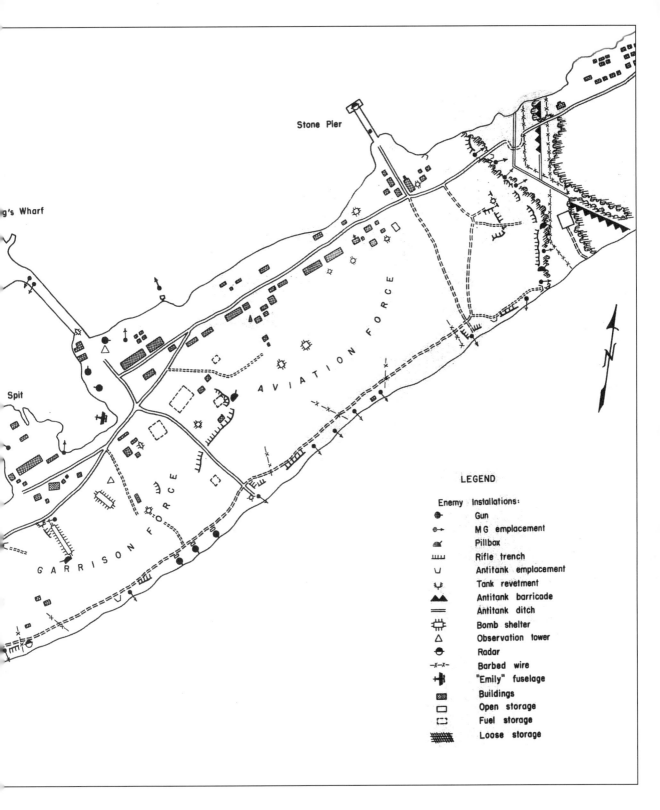

Stone Pier

g's Wharf

Spit

AVIATION FORCE

GARRISON FORCE

LEGEND

Enemy Installations:

Gun	
MG emplacement	
Pillbox	
Rifle trench	
Antitank emplacement	
Tank revetment	
Antitank barricade	
Antitank ditch	
Bomb shelter	
Observation tower	
Radar	
Barbed wire	
"Emily" fuselage	
Buildings	
Open storage	
Fuel storage	
Loose storage	

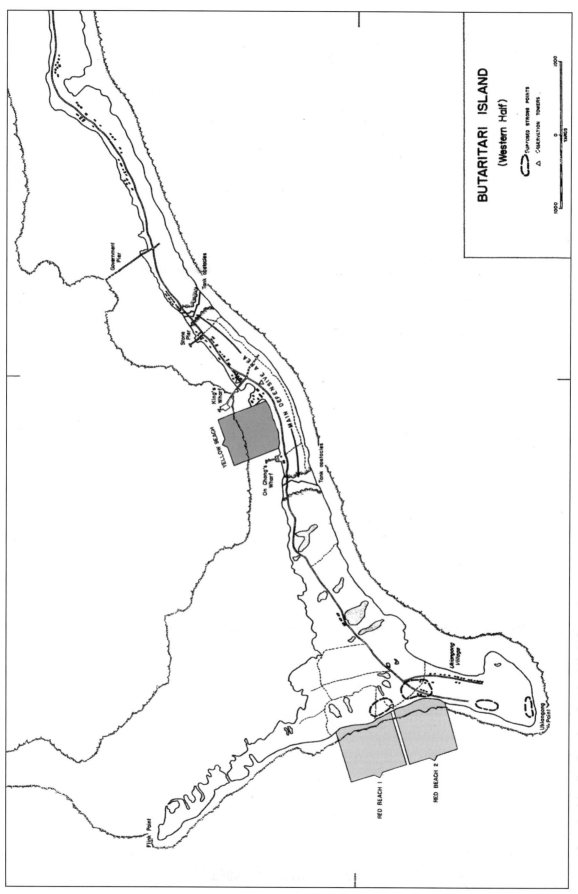

BUTARITARI ISLAND
(Western Half)

⬭ SUPPOSED STRONG POINTS
△ OBSERVATION TOWERS

1000   0   1000
YARDS

Government Pier

Tank obstacles

Stone Pier

King's Wharf

On Chong's Wharf

YELLOW BEACH

MAIN DEFENSIVE AREA

Tank obstacles

Ukiangong Village

Ukiangong Point

RED BEACH 1

RED BEACH 2

Flink Point

Butaritari landing beaches for the US 165th Infantry; D-Day to be 20 November 1943.

Makin Island – LVT-2 drags a pallet of supplies onto the beachhead at Yellow Beach at low tide.

Makin Island – Troops land on Red Beach 1 on the morning of D-Day. Landing craft were able to get right up to the rocky beachhead to discharge their load of tanks (one can be seen in the left background).

(**Opposite, above**) Makin Island – Infantry advance along the main highway towards the west tank barrier.

(**Above**) Makin Island – King's Wharf, partially destroyed prior to the invasion of 20 November. Unlike the situation at Betio, the Japanese did not resist the landings.

(**Above**) Makin Island – Light tanks of C Company, 193rd Tank Battalion, attempt to extract one of their tanks that has sunk in a deep shell hole in the main highway across swamps behind Red Beaches 1 and 2.

(**Right**) Makin Island – Battalion aid station on Yellow Beach. Both army medics and navy corpsmen can be seen hard at work.

(**Opposite**) Makin Island – The 165th Infantry on D+3 march along the lagoon highway past a Japanese Kawanishi flying boat, shot up by Carlson's Raiders back in August 1942 (the remains are still to be seen to this day on Butaritari).

(**Opposite, above**) One of two Japanese Type 95 Ha-Go tanks on Makin (Butaritari). Both were in revetments, but neither was manned or used during the battle.

(**Opposite, below**) One of only three Japanese Rikusentai captured on Makin. Also captured were 101 Korean forced labourers.

(**Left**) Major General Ralph C. Smith, US army, in overall command of the US army's 27th Infantry Division for the assault of Makin Atoll (Butaritari). Due to what appeared to be lack of progress during the battle for Makin, Ralph Smith was to experience first-hand General Holland 'Howling Mad' Smith's temper. It would not be the last time either!

(**Below**) Makin Island – Heavy weapons mortar crews wade ashore on Yellow Beach on D-Day to practically no opposition from the Japanese garrison.

(**Opposite, above**) Makin Island – The 165th Infantry wade ashore early on D-Day to light defensive fire from Japanese machine guns.

(**Opposite, below**) Makin Island – LCVPs circle at the line of departure prior to landing troops on Red Beaches 1 and 2.

(**Above**) Red Beach 1, Makin Island. First waves of troops were boated in LVT-2s.

(**Above**) Makin Island – Airfield construction equipment being offloaded from LSTs at King's Wharf. Planes from the newly-constructed airfield on Butaritari and Tarawa would participate in the capture of the Marshall Islands in early 1944.

(**Right**) Makin Island – M3 'Lee' tanks shell Japanese positions on King's Wharf on D+1.

(**Opposite, above**) Makin Island – Troops of BLT 1 and 3 advance from Red Beaches 1 and 2 on D-Day through torn-up terrain.

(**Opposite, below**) Makin Island – Troops inspect a well-concealed Japanese pillbox near the west tank trap on Butaritari.

Makin Island – Troops from BLT 1 and 2 re-embark on 23/24 November, leaving BLT 3 as a defence battalion on Butaritari.

Chapter Seven

The United States Occupies Makin and Tarawa

Even before Betio had been secured, US Navy Seabees (construction battalions) had landed with their heavy construction equipment to start clearing the all-important airstrip. With the island declared secure, along with the whole of Tarawa, Makin and Apamama shortly after, the clean-up could commence in earnest. Betio was the worst and the Marine Graves Commission began the task of identifying corpses and burying them in one of several graveyard sites all over the island. Little care was taken with the Japanese dead; they were unceremoniously dragged into the open to be dozed into shell holes or into deep water off the south shore. Local labour was used to clear the hundreds of pillboxes, shelters and bunkers.

Within weeks, the Seabees had airstrips on Betio, Makin (Butaritari) and Apamama, ready to receive aircraft. On Betio, the airstrip (Hawkins Field, named for Lieutenant William Deane Hawkins, MOH posthumous) first received navy and Marine fighter squadrons from VF-1 (the newly-contested islands were still receiving Japanese bombing raids from the Marshall Islands well into December 1943).

The 7th USAAF began to transfer aircraft – B24s and B25s – from Funafuti, Ellice Islands. It was soon realized that the runway on Betio was too short for the B24 Liberator bombers, so the Seabees moved further up the Tarawa Atoll from Betio to Bonriki Island where they constructed a much larger airstrip – today's Bonriki International Airport – capable of taking the B24 and B25 bombers. The newly-constructed airstrips on Makin and Apamama were both capable of taking fighters and bombers.

In January 1944, the 7th USAAF moved their headquarters from Funafuti in the Ellice Islands to Bonriki, Tarawa. At the same time they withdrew the B24 and B25 bombers from Betio to Bonriki, leaving only fighters on Betio.

Bombing missions, in particular against the Marshall Islands (the next target in the US 'island-hopping' campaign) began in December 1943 and continued up to the invasion of the Marshall Islands by the US in early 1944. With the fall of the Marshall Islands, the Gilbert and Ellice Islands were deemed to be too far behind the front line, especially as the next target for the assault across the central Pacific was the Mariana

Islands of Saipan, Guam and Tinian, so the 7th USAAF moved bases once again from the Gilbert Islands to the Marianas.

Small garrisons remained on the Gilbert as well as the Ellice Islands until the end of hostilities in the Pacific, under the administration of the newly-appointed British commissioner on Bonriki.

With the end of hostilities with Japan in the Pacific, the US subsequently vacated all their personnel on both the Gilbert and Ellice Islands and administration returned to the British and New Zealand governments until independence in 1979.

(**Below**) The first of eleven cemeteries on Betio. All graves were cleared after the war's end and the remains returned to the US for private burial or interment in the Pacific Cemetery on Hawaii.

(**Opposite, above**) Navy and Marine fighter squadrons on Betio and Bonriki. The runway on Betio proved to be too short for B24 and B25 bombers so they were transferred to Bonriki.

(**Opposite, below**) Hawkins Field, Betio, named after Lieutenant William Deane Hawkins, MOH (Posthumous), KIA Betio, November 1943.

(**Above**) USAAF fighters on the newly-constructed airfield on Butaritari (Makin) Island.

(**Left**) Mechanics work on a .50 calibre nose gun on a B25 Mitchell bomber, watched over by local islanders.

(**Opposite, above**) Hawkins Field, Betio no longer looks like the moonscape it had been only a few weeks earlier, thanks to the Navy Seabees.

(**Opposite, below**) A neatly laid out cemetery on Betio. Unfortunately not every cross had remains beneath it.

Navy Hellcats and B24 Liberators and B25 Mitchells of the 7th USAAF on Bonriki airfield, named Mullinnix Field after Admiral Henry M. Mullinnix, KIA 24 November 1943 on the aircraft carrier *Liscome Bay* off Makin Island.

Appendix I

Casualties

US Marine Casualties

Figures supplied by Casualty Division, Headquarters, US Marine Corps, 5 March 1947:

	Officers	Enlisted
Killed in action	47	790
Wounded, killed	2	32
Died of wounds	8	82
Missing, presumed dead	0	27
Wounded, missing, presumed dead	0	2
Wounded in action	110	2,186
Combat fatigue	1	14
Sub-totals	168	3,133
Grand total		3,301

Japanese Casualties

Strength of Japanese Garrison, 20 November 1943		4,836
Prisoners of War (Japanese) taken	17	
Prisoners of War (Korean labourers) taken	129	
Escaped	0	
	146	−146
Total number of enemy killed on Tarawa		4,690

Strength of Japanese Garrison, Apamama, 20 November	23
Enemy dead, Apamama	−23
Garrison survivors	0

Appendix II

Task Organization

US Task Organizations for the assault and capture of the Gilbert Islands

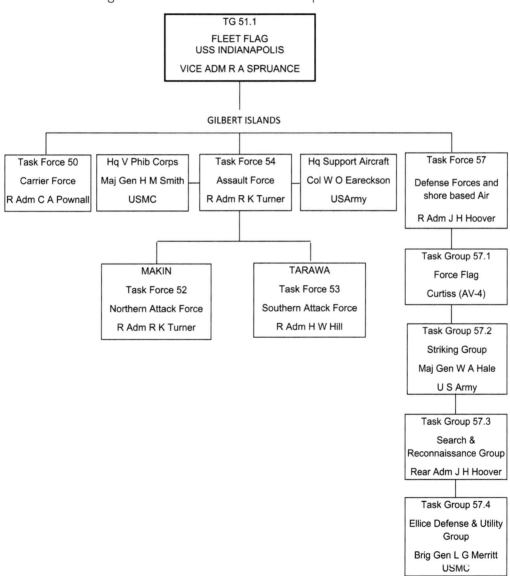

TG 51.1

FLEET FLAG
USS INDIANAPOLIS

VICE ADM R A SPRUANCE

GILBERT ISLANDS

Task Force 50	Hq V Phib Corps	Task Force 54	Hq Support Aircraft	Task Force 57
Carrier Force	Maj Gen H M Smith	Assault Force	Col W O Eareckson	Defense Forces and shore based Air
R Adm C A Pownall	USMC	R Adm R K Turner	USArmy	R Adm J H Hoover

MAKIN

Task Force 52

Northern Attack Force

R Adm R K Turner

TARAWA

Task Force 53

Southern Attack Force

R Adm H W Hill

Task Group 57.1

Force Flag

Curtiss (AV-4)

Task Group 57.2

Striking Group

Maj Gen W A Hale

U S Army

Task Group 57.3

Search &
Reconnaissance Group

Rear Adm J H Hoover

Task Group 57.4

Ellice Defense & Utility
Group

Brig Gen L G Merritt
USMC

Task Force 50 and 53: Operation GALVANIC

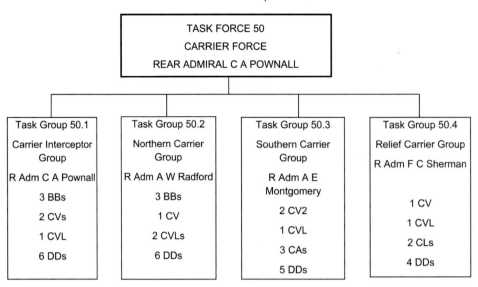

TASK FORCE 50
CARRIER FORCE
REAR ADMIRAL C A POWNALL

Task Group 50.1	Task Group 50.2	Task Group 50.3	Task Group 50.4
Carrier Interceptor Group	Northern Carrier Group	Southern Carrier Group	Relief Carrier Group
R Adm C A Pownall	R Adm A W Radford	R Adm A E Montgomery	R Adm F C Sherman
3 BBs	3 BBs	2 CV2	1 CV
2 CVs	1 CV	1 CVL	1 CVL
1 CVL	2 CVLs	3 CAs	2 CLs
6 DDs	6 DDs	5 DDs	4 DDs

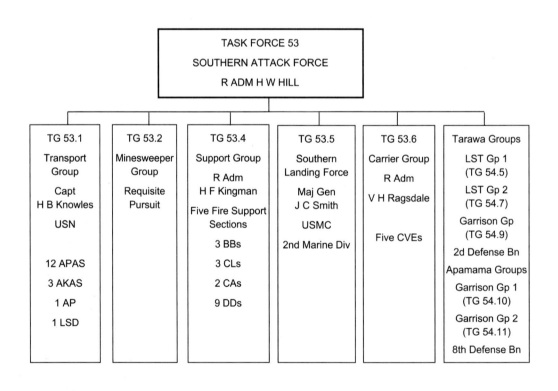

TASK FORCE 53
SOUTHERN ATTACK FORCE
R ADM H W HILL

TG 53.1	TG 53.2	TG 53.4	TG 53.5	TG 53.6	Tarawa Groups
Transport Group	Minesweeper Group	Support Group	Southern Landing Force	Carrier Group	LST Gp 1 (TG 54.5)
Capt H B Knowles	Requisite Pursuit	R Adm H F Kingman	Maj Gen J C Smith	R Adm V H Ragsdale	LST Gp 2 (TG 54.7)
USN		Five Fire Support Sections	USMC		Garrison Gp (TG 54.9)
		3 BBs	2nd Marine Div	Five CVEs	2d Defense Bn
12 APAS		3 CLs			Apamama Groups
3 AKAS		2 CAs			Garrison Gp 1 (TG 54.10)
1 AP		9 DDs			Garrison Gp 2 (TG 54.11)
1 LSD					8th Defense Bn

Task Force 53 and 53.4 Transport and Support Groups: Operation GALVANIC.

Task Force 53 **Capt H B Knowles, USN**	
Trans Div 4	CT 2 (2nd Marines)
APA Zeilin	LT 2/2 (2nd Bn, 2nd Marines)
APA Heywood	LT 2/8 (2nd Bn, 8th Marines)
APA Middleton	LT 3/2 (3rd Bn, 2nd Marines)
APA Biddle	LT Hq/2nd Marines
APA Lee	LT 1/2 (1st Bn, 2nd Marines)
AKA Thuban	Detachments CT 8
Trans Div 18	CT 8 (8th Marines)
APA Monrovia	LT 3/8 (3rd Bn, 8th Marines)
APA Sheridan	LT 1/8 (1st Bn, 8th Marines)
APA La Salle	Division Troops
APA Doyen	Division Troops
AKA Virgo	Detachments CT 8
LSD Ashland	Medium Tanks
(joined transport group at Vila Harbor, Efate)	
Trans Div 6	CT 6 (6th Marines)
APA Harris	LT 3/6 (3rd Bn, 6th Marines)
APA Bell	LT 2/6 (2nd Bn, 6th Marines)
APA Ormsby	LT Hq/6th Marines
APA Feland	LT 1/6 (1st Bn, 6th Marines)
AKA Bellatrix	Detachments CT 6

Task Force 53.4 **Rear Adm H F Kingman**	
Fire Support Section 1	
Tennessee	BB 43
Mobile	CL 63
Birmingham	CL 62
Bailey	DD 492
Frazer	DD 607
Fire Support Section 2	
Maryland	BB 46
Santa Fe	CL 60
Gansevoort	DD 608
Meade	DD 602
Fire Support Section 3	
Colorado	BB 45
Portland	CA 33
Anderson	DD 411
Russell	DD 414
Fire Support Section 4	
Ringgold	DD 500
Dashiell	DD 659
Fire Support Section 5	
Indianapolis	CA 35
Schroeder	DD 501

Japanese Garrison Force Organization as of 20 November 1943.

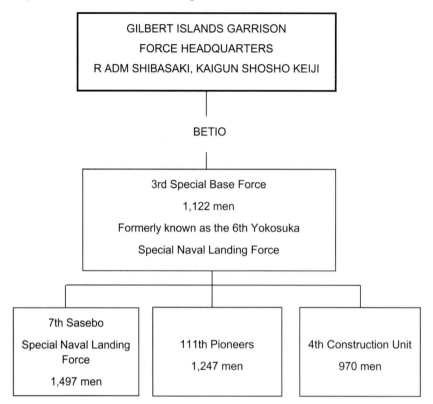

GILBERT ISLANDS GARRISON
FORCE HEADQUARTERS
R ADM SHIBASAKI, KAIGUN SHOSHO KEIJI

BETIO

3rd Special Base Force

1,122 men

Formerly known as the 6th Yokosuka

Special Naval Landing Force

7th Sasebo
Special Naval Landing
Force
1,497 men

111th Pioneers
1,247 men

4th Construction Unit
970 men